60c

Past-into-Present Series

SCOTLAND

R D Lobban

B T BATSFORD LTD London

First published 1974

Computer composition by
Eyre & Spottiswoode Ltd at Grosvenor Press, Portsmouth
and printed by The Anchor Press, Tiptree, Essex
for the publisher
B T Batsford Ltd, 4 Fitzhardinge Street, London W1A 0AH

ISBN 0 7134 2834 1

Acknowledgments

The author and Publishers would like to thank the following for the photographs used in this book: Department of the Environment for figs 2, 3, 5, 7, 21; Central Office of Information for fig 4; Aerofilms for figs 9, 35; Mansell Collection for figs 10, 12, 13, 16, 17, 19, 23, 26, 27, 29, 30, 34, 37, 39, 44, 46, 50; Trustees of the Victoria and Albert Museum for fig 18; Radio Times Hulton Picture Library for figs 51, 52, 53, 55, 56, 57; Keystone for figs 54, 58, 61, 62, 63; Popperfoto for figs 59, 60, 65. The other pictures appearing in this book are the property of the Publishers.

Contents

The Illustrations

1. The Union of Peoples

For about 6,000 years men have lived in the country we now call Scotland. Through the centuries, a rich tapestry of different peoples have settled there and made their homes. They came to a beautiful land with widely varying regions, and scenery which ranged from the mountains, lochs and glens of the Highlands, the fertile fields of the Lowlands and east coast plain, to the rolling hills of the Southern Uplands. Throughout the long years these enduring features of the landscape have been closely interwoven with the lives, fortunes and tragedies of the people of Scotland, and against this magnificent backcloth a wonderful history has been unfolded.

First settlers

Up until about 8,000 BC Scotland was covered with the great ice sheets of the last Ice Age, but slowly thereafter the ice began to retreat northwards. Somewhere about 6,000 BC the melting of the ice caps helped to form the English Channel and so separate the British Isles from the Continent. Slowly the climate improved, and sometime before 4,000 BC, the first small groups of people made their appearance in Scotland. These settlers, the first inhabitants of Scotland, lived as primitive hunters and fishers on various coastal sites. They hunted deer and wild cattle with crude stone weapons, and when seals or whales were stranded on the shore, they hacked them up for meat and blubber.

1 Typical Highland scenery — Beinn MacDhui.

Farming

Somewhere about 3,000 BC, a second group of people arrived from the Continent and established settlements in many parts of the country. These newcomers introduced agriculture into Scotland. Some of them were farmers who cultivated cereal crops with stone tools and an ox-drawn plough, while others concentrated on rearing their herds of cattle, pigs, sheep and goats. Something of their lives can be learned from the remains of a settlement constructed at Skara Brae in Orkney, in about 2,000 BC. The huts and furnishings there were made of stone, and for long centuries they were covered

2 House at Skara Brae, showing hearth, box bed, dresser, tanks and quernstones.

and preserved by a blanket of sand.

The most common dwelling-place at Skara Brae was a small one-roomed stone hut with immensely thick walls. To the right and left of the entrance were two stone-framed bed-boxes, one measuring 6ft 6in (195cm) in length and the other 5ft 2in (155cm). There was a stone hearth in the middle of the earthen floor, and opposite the door a stone dresser with stone shelves and uprights. There were also watertight clay boxes on the floor, perhaps for storing live fish or lobsters. The roof was made of stretched skins, or divots, supported by rafters of whalebone or driftwood.

The weather in Orkney could be cold and stormy, and to provide protection from the fierce gales the inhabitants of Skara Brae used to pile up their ashes and refuse around their houses. Small passageways were left between the huts, but in time these, too, were roofed over with rubbish. Eventually only the tops of the huts were left uncovered, and the settlement looked like a huge mound with the rounded tips of the roofs jutting out.

Beaker people

Shortly after 2,000 BC, a new group of settlers began arriving in Scotland from across the North Sea. These people have become known to historians as the Beaker People, because of the pottery vessels or 'beakers' which they used. They introduced copper and bronze tools and weapons to Scotland, and over the next thousand years a flourishing trade in bronze metal-work was developed throughout the country.

The Celts

Sometime after 200 BC, a fourth group of people known as the Celts made their appearance in Scotland. The Celts originally hailed from the Upper Danube in Germany, and had settled in many lands in Western Europe. It was the Celts who introduced iron-working into Scotland, and over the next few hundred years they extended their control over the whole country. Some of the earlier inhabitants were probably forced to live as lower and inferior people under their new Celtic overlords.

3 Dun Carloway Broch, with later dwellings in the foreground.

8

By AD 100 Scotland was divided into a number of tribal areas occupied by various tribes. Normally each tribe would have a capital town, or *oppidum*, like Traprain Law in East Lothian, the *oppidum* of the Votadini tribe. Traprain Law was situated on the top of a small hill. It covered an area of about 32 acres (13 hectares), and was enclosed by a stone wall. The inhabitants lived in small round houses made of wattle and daub, and most of them were farmers working the fields on the lower slopes of the hill. The *oppidum* was also a market centre, and tribesmen came from the surrounding area to buy and sell goods.

The Celts were great warriors, and there were frequent inter-tribal wars. They fought with chariots drawn by two small horses, and charioteers held an honoured position in the tribe. All this fighting made life dangerous and uncertain. To protect themselves the Celts built great fortifications known as duns, brochs and crannogs. Duns were round or D-shaped stone-walled structures situated on rocks or hill-tops; brochs were round towers with two thicknesses of walls and narrow galleries between; while crannogs were fortified villages built on wooden uprights above the waters of a loch.

The Romans

Towards the end of the first century AD, the Celtic tribes in Scotland found themselves threatened by the Romans. The Romans had built up a great Empire, and in AD 43 they sent an army to invade and conquer Britain. About AD 80 the Roman general Julius Agricola advanced into Scotland, and constructed a great fortress at Inchtuthill, 15 miles (24 km) north of Perth. In AD 84 he pushed on northwards, and in a great battle at an unknown site named Mons Graupius he defeated his enemies under their leader, Calgacus.

Soon afterwards, however, the Romans were forced to withdraw troops from Britain in order to defend other parts of their Empire. They therefore abandoned most of Scotland and concentrated their forces in a fort at Newstead on the Tweed. About AD 100 this fort, too, was abandoned. Later, in about AD 120 a great line of fortifications known as Hadrian's Wall was built to stretch from the Solway to the Tyne. This became the northern frontier of the Romans in Britain. In 142, the Romans gathered their forces and again pushed north. They erected an earthen rampart and line of fortifications known as the Antonine Wall between the Forth and Clyde. This line they held for about 50 years, but then they withdrew once more to Hadrian's Wall. The Emperor Severus led a punitive expedition into Scotland between 209 and 211, but thereafter Scotland remained undisturbed by the Roman forces.

In the main, therefore, Scotland lay outside the Roman province of Britain with its towns, amphitheatres and other features of Roman civilization. The southern part of the country, however, did experience a military occupation, and the tribes there traded with the Roman forts and merchants. Roman coins, brooches and other objects, for instance, have been discovered at Traprain Law, and Latin alphabet slabs were even in use there. Obviously the tribes in Scotland would gain a great deal from their contact with the Romans, and they might have adopted some of their ways and customs.

By the fifth century, Roman power was weakening throughout their great

4 View of Hadrian's Wall.

Empire. In Britain the tribes from the north of Scotland and from Ireland were launching frequent attacks against Hadrian's Wall, and on several occasions they broke through into the Roman province. At length, in AD 410, the legions were withdrawn, and Roman rule in Britain ended.

Early kingdoms

The situation in Scotland in the years after the departure of the Romans was a rather confused one. To the north, beyond the Forth and the Clyde, was the kingdom of the Picts, a mysterious group of people who may have obtained their name from the Romans' custom of calling them *Picti* or 'painted ones'. They have left us a valuable artistic legacy in the form of several beautifully sculptured stone slabs decorated with intricate designs, animal symbols and hunting scenes. Traces of their language also survive in the prefix 'Pit' ('manor', farm-stead) found in many place names throughout the area they occupied (Pitlochry, Pittodrie etc.).

South of the Forth and Clyde were several tribal kingdoms belonging to the Britons, a Celtic people akin to the Britons in England and Wales. One of the most important of these was Strathclyde which stretched along the Clyde valley from Loch Lomond to the Solway Firth and beyond, and which had its capital at Dumbarton. To the west in Argyll and the islands was Dalriada, the kingdom of the Scots. The Scots were a Celtic people from Ireland, and they had begun settling in southern Argyll during the fourth and fifth centuries AD. The Scots were to give their name to the country, and their language was the ancestor of Gaelic, the language of the Highlands and for a time of the Scottish court.

During the sixth century a Germanic people, the Angles, were added to this conglomeration of peoples. England had been invaded by the Anglo-Saxons from Germany in the fifth century, and now the Angles began moving into

5 Designs on the sculptured stone at Glamis.

parts of south-east Scotland. They established a kingdom known as Lothian, and for a time in the seventh century they even penetrated across the Forth and occupied Fife. In AD 685, however, they were defeated by the Picts in a battle at Nechtansmere in Angus, and their advance was halted.

Christianity

Over the next few centuries, the Picts, Scots, Angles and Britons were engaged in many bitter struggles against each other. From an early date, however, strong bonds were also being forged between them as Christianity slowly spread throughout the land. One of the first missionaries to come to Scotland was St Ninian who set up a church at Whithorn in Galloway towards the end of the

6 Ruins of a medieval nunnery on the island of Iona.

11

fourth century. Another famous missionary was St Columba who came from Ireland in 563 to set up a monastery on the island of Iona. Iona became a great centre of Christianity in Scotland, and throughout the centuries Scotsmen have regarded it with reverence and awe.

Some wonderful tales have been told of the deeds and determination of these early missionaries. Here, for instance, is a description of St Columba's first encounter with King Brude of the Picts:

> On the Saint's first laborious journey to King Brude, it happened that the King, swollen by royal pride, acted arrogantly, and did not open his castle gates upon the blessed man's first arrival. As soon as the man of God saw this he went with his comrades to the openings of the gates, and, first pressing on them an image of the Lord's cross, he then laid his hand upon them, striking against the gates; and immediately, of their own accord, the bolts were forcibly withdrawn, and the gates opened with all speed. Learning this, the King and his council were much afraid; and he left the house, and went to meet the blessed man with reverence; and thenceforth from that day all the days of his life the same ruler honoured the holy and venerable man befittingly with very high esteem.

An equally fascinating legend is told about St Moluag, one of Columba's contemporaries. He and St Columba were great rivals, and on one occasion they were racing their curraghs (boats) towards the island of Lismore for the honour of being the first missionary to land. Steadily St Columba drew ahead, and it seemed that he must be the victor, but St Moluag would not admit defeat. Grimly he drew forth his sword, and with a fierce stroke he cut off his little finger. Then he flung the finger on to the shore before Columba's boat had grounded, and so was able to claim the island as his own particular mission field.

The Vikings

For some centuries, missionaries from Iona and other centres spread Christianity throughout Scotland. Then, towards the end of the eighth century, fierce raiders or Vikings from Norway and Denmark began to raid the Scottish coast. In 795, Iona itself was sacked, and many other areas on the islands and the mainland were devastated. The Vikings also established many settlements in Scotland, and they secured control of Orkney and Shetland, Sutherland, Caithness and the Hebrides. They formed an important new element in the population of these areas, and from their language have come many Scottish personal and place names.

Unification of Scotland

Despite the terrible sufferings they inflicted on the people of Scotland, the Vikings did in a strange way help to bring about the unification of the country. Their attacks seem to have so weakened the Picts that in 844 they accepted Kenneth MacAlpin, King of the Scots, as their ruler. The new kingdom was known as Alba, and included most of Scotland north of the Forth and Clyde.

The kingdoms of southern Scotland were added to Alba early in the eleventh century. In 1018, Malcolm II of Alba defeated the Northumbrians at Carham on the Tweed, and Lothian became part of his kingdom. In the same year Malcolm's grandson, Duncan, was made King of Strathclyde. When in due course Duncan succeeded to the throne of Alba in 1034, the whole mainland of Scotland was united under his rule. The ruling house of the Scots had played a leading part in this unifying movement, and it was their name that was given to the new kingdom.

Queen Margaret

Some years later, in 1070, Malcolm III (known as Canmore or 'Big Head') married an English princess, Margaret. She had taken refuge in Scotland after William of Normandy's conquest of England in 1066, but she considered the Scots backward and uncivilized. During her reign, she strove hard to introduce English ways and customs into the country. Before this time, Gaelic had been the main language of Scotland, but Margaret never learned it and increasingly English became the language of the court and government. She also introduced reforms into the Scottish Church, and encouraged the building of a great abbey at Dunfermline. Queen Margaret and her husband were buried there, and later when she was made a saint it became a famous place of pilgrimage.

7 Dunfermline Abbey — the shrine of Queen Margaret.

David I: the Normans

Malcolm Canmore and Queen Margaret died within a few days of each other in 1094, and after their deaths there was a period of confusion as rival claimants struggled for the throne. At length, in 1124, one of their sons succeeded as King David I. During his reign (1124-53) a new people, the Normans, began to make their way into Scotland. David had spent many years in England, and had developed close ties with the Norman rulers there. He himself held lands in England as the Earl of Huntingdon, and when he succeeded to the Scottish throne he brought many of his English tenants north and gave them estates in Scotland. The old Celtic and Scottish nobility were pushed out, and Norman families like the Bruces, Lindsays and Fitzallans took their place and married their heiresses.

With the Normans came a much more efficient system of government. Great nobles were appointed as sheriffs to rule each district, and the king's justice brought law and order to all parts of the country. The Norman lords also built castles to control their lands, and introduced the feudal system into Scotland. Thus the nobles held their lands from the king in return for their fealty and service; they in turn let out holdings to their followers, and in return these followers fought for them and the king. At the bottom of the social scale were the peasants who provided their lords with produce and labour in return for their plots of land. Some peasants were freemen, but large numbers were serfs who could not leave their lands without their lord's permission. Some were even forced to wear iron collars showing to which lord they belonged.

Most of the peasants and people of Scotland at this time lived in little hamlets known as touns. These were small settlements of between 8 and 10 families who farmed the surrounding land in common. They lived in small crudely-built stone cottages roofed with turf or thatch. Holes in the walls and roof served as windows and chimneys, while the furniture consisted of rough beds of heather and a few wooden benches and chests. Often the animals were kept in a small section of the cottage which was only separated from the living quarters by a small internal wall.

The lands round the toun were divided into the infield and outfield, the infield consisting of the more fertile land close to the hamlet, and the outfield being made up of patches of the poorer and more distant land. The infield received all the available manure, and it was ploughed with a heavy wooden plough drawn by 8 or 12 oxen. Each householder contributed one or two oxen to a plough team, and he would be allocated several strips or rigs scattered through the various fields for growing his oats and barley. Cattle and sheep were usually grazed on the outfield or on rough pastureland. In some areas, though, during the summer months, they might be taken to graze up in the hills. The touns were practically self-sufficient, and only such commodities as salt and iron were obtained from outside.

During David I's reign (1124-53), several towns or burghs were founded. Those founded by the King himself included Stirling, Perth, Aberdeen and Edinburgh, and were known as royal burghs. Flemish craftsmen and merchants were brought to Scotland to live and work in the burghs. As trade and commerce expanded, the burghs became centres for new ideas. Other import-

8 The ruins of Melrose Abbey which was founded by David I in 1136.

ant centres of progress were the monasteries founded by King David at such places as Melrose, Kelso, Jedburgh and Holyrood. Some of them grazed huge herds of sheep, and they added considerably to the wealth and prosperity of the kingdom.

A Golden Age

During the century after the death of David I in 1153, and particularly during the reigns of William the Lion (1165-1214), Alexander II (1214-49), and Alexander III (1249-86), Scotland continued to make steady progress. New burghs such as Glasgow, Ayr and Peebles were founded, and the country gradually became more settled. Over the years the various districts and regions that had formerly been separate kingdoms were welded into the one country and kingdom of Scotland. In 1266, too, the work of unification was advanced a stage further when the Hebrides were taken over from the King of Norway. Most of the people in Scotland were still very poor, but so peaceful were these years to seem to later and more troubled generations that they were often looked upon as the Golden Age.

2. The Struggle for Independence

Although Scotland had been making steady progress during the thirteenth and fourteenth centuries, she still had not established an entirely satisfactory relationship with the powerful kingdom of England that lay to her south. For many years Malcolm Canmore and his successors attempted to extend their frontiers to the Tyne, and it was only in the reign of Malcolm IV (1153-65) that the Scottish kings finally abandoned their claim to Northumberland, Westmoreland and Cumberland.

Many of the English kings, for their part, had ambitions of gaining control of Scotland. They were the overlords of the Scottish monarchs for the lands they held in England, and some of them wished to extend this overlordship to cover the Scottish kings' lands in Scotland itself. When William the Lion was captured near Alnwick while invading England in 1174, for instance, he was forced to do homage for all his possessions to Henry II before he was released. Some years later, in 1189, Richard I sold these rights back to the Scots in return for a large sum of money to equip a Crusade, but the English claims to overlordship over Scotland were never completely abandoned.

Edward I and Scotland

Such claims were to be pushed forward much more aggressively by Edward I after the death of the Scottish King Alexander III in 1286. Alexander was only 44 when his horse stumbled and he was thrown over a cliff at Kinghorn in Fife. He was succeeded by his grand-daughter Margaret, the daughter of the King of Norway. Edward I had already conquered Wales, and now he saw an opportunity of uniting the British Isles under his rule. In 1287, therefore, he made an agreement with the Norwegian King that the six-year-old Margaret should marry his five-year-old son Edward. The Scottish barons gave their approval to the marriage, and it seemed as if the two countries would inevitably be drawn together.

Unfortunately for Edward's plans, however, the Maid of Norway died in the Orkney Islands as she was journeying to Scotland. There was now no obvious successor, and in all 13 claimants came forward, including two prominent Scottish noblemen, Robert Bruce, Lord of Annandale, and John Balliol, Lord of Badenoch. The Scottish nobles were afraid that a civil war would break out, and they therefore invited Edward I to act as arbitrator. Edward summoned them to Norham on the Tweed in 1291, and before making his decision he insisted that the claimants should recognize him as overlord of Scotland. Eventually all agreed, and in 1292 Edward announced that Balliol had the best claim. Balliol then swore an oath of fealty to Edward and was crowned king at Scone.

It now seemed that Edward had secured his objectives, for Balliol was a weak ruler and ready to do as he was told. But the English King then acted rashly, and proceeded to insult and humiliate the unfortunate Balliol. He even summoned him to London to explain why he had not paid a wine bill owed to an English merchant by Alexander III. Finally, in 1295, he ordered Balliol to provide men and money for a war against France. This was too much for the Scottish nobles and clergy. They urged and persuaded Balliol to defy Edward and to make a treaty of alliance with the King of France. This treaty marked the beginning of the 'Auld Alliance' between Scotland and France which lasted for over 250 years.

Edward was enraged by the defiance of the Scots, and he determined to teach them a terrible lesson. In 1296, he led a great army against the town of Berwick, and slaughtered most of its inhabitants. He then defeated the Scottish army at Dunbar, and soon had subdued the whole country. English garrisons were placed in all the important Scottish castles, and English officials took over the running of the country. To show that the independence of Scotland was finally ended, Edward carried Balliol off into captivity and transferred the ancient Scottish Coronation Stone from Scone to Westminster Abbey.

9 A view of Berwick on Tweed, the early Scottish royal burgh which was seized by the English.

William Wallace

Scotland now seemed utterly crushed, but once again Edward had miscalculated. The Scottish nobles and clergy had sworn an oath of loyalty to him, but most of the Scottish people bitterly resented the English occupation. Very soon small bands of determined men under leaders like Andrew of Moray and William Wallace were organizing armed resistance against the English invaders. Wallace was the son of Sir Malcolm Wallace of Elderslie in Renfrewshire. He first became prominent when he was involved in a quarrel with English soldiers in Lanark and killed the English sheriff there. He now took up arms against the English, and within a short time men from all over the country were coming to join him in his attacks on English castles and strongholds.

In 1297, Wallace learned that a large English army was advancing towards Stirling, and with Andrew of Moray he moved his forces there to oppose it. He took up a position on the north bank of the River Forth with the much larger English army opposite on the south bank. Confidently the English commanders ordered their forces forward to cross the wooden bridge that spanned the river. Immediately Wallace saw his opportunity. He waited until about half of the enemy had crossed, and then gave the signal for attack. The Scottish spearsmen charged upon the English van, while the right wing raced across to hold the bridge and cut off any retreat. Helplessly, the English soldiers on the south bank watched as their comrades were overwhelmed. Soon they panicked, and the English army fled away to the south. Wallace and his men pursued them and drove them out of the country.

Edward I was not the person to accept such a defeat lightly, and in 1298 he himself led a great army north into Scotland. Wallace retreated from the Border counties and laid them waste. In this way, the English were not able to obtain the provisions they needed. His tactics might have succeeded, but informers told Edward that Wallace and his men were lying in wait at Falkirk. Swiftly the

10 Statue of Sir William Wallace at Stirling.

English King marched against the Scots before they could withdraw.

Wallace's army was much smaller than Edward's, and at the very beginning of the battle his tiny force of cavalry fled from the field. The Scots infantry were drawn up in the famous schiltron formations with the 12ft (360cm) long spears of the Scots spearsmen bristling out in all directions. Repeatedly the schiltrons threw back the charges of the English cavalry, but the Scots had no answer when Edward brought up his longbowmen. The English arrows wreaked terrible havoc in the Scottish lines, and only a very few men including Wallace were able to escape from the field.

Once again, Scotland lay at the mercy of the 'Hammer of the Scots' (the grim nickname bestowed by later generations on Edward I of England), and English troops re-occupied the country and garrisoned the castles. The Scottish nobles quickly made their peace, and Wallace became a hunted outlaw. In 1305, he was betrayed by a certain Sir John Menteith, and was taken to London for trial. He was found guilty of treason and sentenced to a horrible death. His head was placed on London Bridge, and parts of his body were displayed at Newcastle, Berwick, Perth and Stirling, as a grim warning to any other Scots who might think of following his example.

Robert Bruce

Within a year, however, a new Scottish leader had appeared in the person of Robert Bruce. Bruce's ancestors had been given lands in Scotland by David I, and his grandfather had been a claimant for the throne after the death of the Maid of Norway. Bruce now saw his opportunity. In 1306, he arranged a meeting with one of his rivals, John Comyn, in a church in Dumfries, to discuss their plans. A fierce quarrel broke out, and Bruce and his followers killed the unfortunate Comyn. This act of sacrilege resulted in Bruce's excommunication, and the enmity of Comyn's family and friends. Thus, when he was crowned King at Scone a few weeks later, only a small number of his own followers were there to support him.

His early campaigns, too, were quite disastrous. His small army was defeated by the English near Perth, and then he was hounded throughout the western counties both by the English and by the relatives of John Comyn. He became a hunted fugitive and eventually was forced to withdraw from the mainland and take refuge on Rathlin, an island off the coast of Ireland.

Most men would have abandoned the struggle after such setbacks, but Bruce now proved himself one of the most resolute and determined of men. He crossed back to the mainland and began waging a skilful and effective campaign of guerrilla warfare. His prospects improved when Edward I died in 1307, and steadily he began to win more support. Soon he had control of the countryside, and the English garrisons were safe only in their strongholds and castles.

Bruce had no proper siege engines with which to attack the castles, but in a series of brilliant and ingenious manoeuvres, he and his chief lieutenants, Sir James Douglas and Thomas Randolph, Earl of Moray, managed to gain possession of the major strongholds. Linlithgow Castle was captured when a hay cart full of Scottish soldiers was jammed in the gateway; Roxburgh was taken when Douglas's men, holding their cloaks tightly around them, were

19

11 Stirling Castle — a strategic stronghold during the Wars of Independence.

mistaken for cattle by the sentries; and Edinburgh was seized by Randolph's men when a former member of the garrison remembered a secret path up the castle rock.

By 1313, only Stirling and Bothwell Castles remained in the hands of the English, and at last Edward II was roused to action. In 1314, he moved into Scotland with a huge army of over 20,000 men to relieve the garrison at Stirling. Bruce had only about 7,000 men to oppose the English advance, but he took up a strong defensive position in the marshy lands near the rivers Bannock and Forth, and blocked the route to Stirling. Foolishly, Edward encamped on this boggy land, and in so doing presented Bruce with a golden opportunity.

On the morning of 24 June 1314, Bruce ordered his army into the attack. His cavalry drove off the English archers, and then to the astonishment of King Edward he sent forward his infantry against the huge English army. The English cavalry charged against the advancing Scots, but the forest of spears threw them back. Steadily the Scots moved forward, and all the while the English were being forced back into a small, confined space between the rivers Bannock and Forth. Now they had no room to manoeuvre nor to mount a charge, and at last they broke as the relentless Scottish advance continued. Edward managed to escape, but countless thousands of his men were slaughtered or were drowned in the Bannock or the Forth.

Bruce had won a great and decisive victory at Bannockburn, and Scotland was at last free from the invaders. For a number of years after Bannockburn, fighting did in fact continue between the Scots and the English, but in 1328 a

12 Statue of Robert Bruce at Stirling.

treaty was signed at Northampton. By this the English agreed to recognize Scotland as an independent kingdom, and Robert Bruce as its King.

The successful struggle of the Scots to win their freedom was an epic achievement, and it is one of the first examples in Europe of a small country waging a campaign for national independence. During the course of the long struggle, the various peoples of Scotland were welded into a real nation, and the country was finally united under its warrior king. The principles for which they fought and the spirit which sustained them were most admirably expressed in 1320 in a document known as the Declaration of Arbroath. It was sent by the Scottish nobles to the Pope in Rome asking him to recognize the independence of Scotland:

> For so long as an hundred remain alive we are minded never a whit to bow beneath the yoke of English dominion. It is not for glory, riches or honours that we fight; it is for liberty alone, the liberty which no good man relinquishes but with his life.

The problems of independence

Like many modern countries which have won their independence, however, the Scots quickly found themselves faced with daunting and sometimes overwhelming problems. The country had been devastated during the wars, and it now needed strong leadership and a period of peace and stability. Unfortunately, Robert Bruce died in 1329, just one year after the Treaty of Northampton, and was succeeded by his son, David II, a mere boy of eight.

Almost at once the land lapsed into disorder and anarchy as rival barons sought to extend their power, and the descendants of John Balliol attempted to regain the throne. In 1333, Edward III of England intervened with a strong army, and after defeating the Scots at Halidon Hill he ravaged and laid waste to the countryside. Later, in 1346, David II invaded England, but he was defeated and captured, and a huge ransom had to be raised to secure his release. Then, as if to complete the picture of disaster and doom, the dreaded plague, the Black Death, spread north from England in 1349, killing perhaps a quarter of the country's total population.

The same sorry story continued throughout the remainder of the fourteenth century. A new royal family, the Stewarts, came to the throne in 1371, but none of the kings was strong enough to rule the country and keep the nobles under control. Indeed, many of the nobles lived as though they were independent princes. Some of the great families like the Douglases, who had supported Bruce during the Wars of Independence, had been rewarded with large estates. In subsequent years the Douglases added considerably to their possessions, and by the end of the fourteenth century they had huge territories ranging through Douglasdale, Annandale, Clydesdale, Galloway, Stirling, Lothian and Moray. They could raise a fighting force of thousands of men, and on the Borders they carried on a private feud with the English Earls of Northumberland.

During the fifteenth century, the various kings of Scotland did make serious attempts to reduce the powers of the nobles, and frequently acted boldly and ruthlessly against them. James I (1406-37), for instance, summoned a group of Highland chiefs to a parliament at Inverness, and then seized and executed a number of them. Afterwards he wrote a poem to celebrate his actions:

> To the dungeon strong
> Haul the wretches along.
> As in Christ's my hope
> They deserve the rope.

James II (1437-60) was equally ruthless. At a dinner party in Stirling Castle, he stabbed the Earl of Douglas to death, and then proceeded to destroy the Douglases' castles and to lay waste to their lands. Such actions, however, were never decisive, for no king survived long enough to complete his work. All died at a relatively early age and were succeeded by minors. During the ensuing regencies, the nobles would recover any powers they had lost during the previous reign.

Scotland's experience of independence during the fourteenth and fifteenth centuries had not, therefore, been an entirely happy one. Nevertheless, the picture was not all bleak and gloomy. In the government of the country important new institutions such as Parliament and the Session Court were being developed, while vital advances in education had been secured with the founding of St Andrew's University in 1412 and Glasgow University in 1451. Some fine poetry and literature was also produced during the reign of James III (1460-88). Clearly, Scotland was sharing in the general advance of European

13 Margaret of Denmark, wife of James III.

civilization, and this small northern kingdom was being influenced by the swelling currents of European culture and learning.

Life of the people

For the ordinary people, these eventful years during the fourteenth and fifteenth centuries also produced many changes. Many suffered terribly during the long struggles for independence, but they also secured several real benefits. The great disturbances and upheavals loosened the control of the lords over their peasants, and by the fourteenth century serfdom had practically disappeared in Scotland. The ravages of war, moreover, were soon made good, since the simple cottages could quickly be replaced. There was little real improvement in the system of farming, however — in the touns, the centuries-old infield-outfield system was maintained with little change.

Nevertheless, Scotland was making some significant economic progress in these years. The number of burghs had steadily increased, and they were playing an important part in the country's affairs. The burgesses had a monopoly of foreign trade, and had established profitable trade connections with many European countries. Scottish merchants were to be found in Scandinavia, Poland, Germany, France and the Low Countries, and Scottish hides, wool and fish were being exported to all these countries. In exchange, wine from France and fine cloth from Flanders were being brought to Scotland to add some comfort and even luxury to the lives of the great nobles. and merchants.

23

14 A fourteenth-century grain mill at East Linton in East Lothian.

Despite their growing importance, however, the Scottish burghs were still relatively small at the end of the fifteenth century. Most of the burgesses were either merchants or craftsmen, but many of them also still grew crops on the burgh lands surrounding the town. The burgh was entered by way of the ports or gates, and all the life and activity of the place seemed to be centred on the main thoroughfare or High Gate. There was situated the Kirk, the Mercat Cross where all the important announcements were made, the Tron Gate for weighing goods, and the Tolbooth where prisoners were kept and taxes paid. Most of the houses in the High Gate or on the streets or wynds running off it were built of stone, and some substantial 2- or 3-storeyed buildings were to be seen. Everything had a rather untidy appearance — stalls and stairs were erected in front of houses, many potholes left between the flat paving stones on the High Gate, and great heaps of midden rubbish strewn all around. But all the time there was a bustle and a gaiety about these early Scottish burghs, and new ideas, habits and fashions were continually being brought in from France and other Continental countries by sailors and merchants.

3. Reform and Reformation

James IV

The progress and advances that had been evident during the reign of James III were carried on and expanded under his son, James IV (1488-1513). The Renaissance with its revival of learning and the arts was influencing many countries of Western Europe, and James was determined that Scotland should not be left behind. He founded a College of Surgeons in Edinburgh and a third university at Aberdeen, while in 1496 an act was passed ordering all barons and freeholders to send their eldest sons to school when they were 'eight or nine years and to remain there till they have perfect Latin'. There was also a marked flourishing of Scottish literature led by such writers as William Dunbar and Robert Henryson. Their works could now reach a much wider public, for the King allowed two merchants named Chapman and Myllar to set up Scotland's first printing press in Edinburgh.

James was also interested in scientific experiments, and he gave encouragement and support to several inventors. One of his favourites was an Italian who was trying to find some method of flying: 'An Italian took in hand to fly with wings, and to that effect he made a pair of wings of feathers, which being fastened upon him, he flew off the castle wall of Stirling; but shortly he fell to the ground and broke his thigh-bone; but the blame thereof he ascribed to that there was some hen feathers in the wings, which yearned and coveted the midden and not the skies.'

James also adopted strong measures to establish law and order in his kingdom. Royal justiciars were sent round the country, and in the Border counties he set up special courts at Jedburgh and other towns to deal with law-breakers. He also set about bringing the Highlands under his control, but here he experienced much greater difficulties. The development of the clan system from the thirteenth century onwards gave tremendous power to the chiefs, and some of them ruled their lands as if they themselves were kings or princes. Most powerful of all were the MacDonalds. From the middle of the fourteenth century, their chiefs began to call themselves the Lords of the Isles. In 1411, a Lord of the Isles claimed the Earldom of Ross and led an army towards Aberdeen, but he was defeated at the Battle of Harlaw and forced to retreat.

In an attempt to curb the over-powerful Highland chiefs, James led six expeditions to the West Highlands. In 1493, he abolished the title of Lord of the Isles, and in the following years he established a number of strongholds in the Highlands. To maintain royal authority in the area, he gave increased powers to the Earl of Argyll, chief of the Campbells, and the Earl of Huntly, chief of the Gordons, authorizing them to act as royal lieutenants.

James the fourt
Began his Rayne
1489 He maried
Margaret eldest dochter
of Henry the sebinth

15 James IV and Margaret Tudor.

During his reign, James sought to strengthen Scotland's defences by building a navy. The pride of his fleet was the 240-ft (73-metre) long *Great Michael* which had over 20 guns and carried 1,000 fighting men. The Scottish navy was involved in a few skirmishes with English privateers. Then, for a time, more peaceful relations with England were established when in 1503 James married Margaret Tudor, the daughter of Henry VII. Unfortunately this new policy did not last very long, and when England under Henry VIII joined in a war against France, the French King asked James IV for assistance. James hesitated, but he could not resist the appeal to his sense of chivalry — the Queen of France had sent him a turquoise ring and a letter naming him as her champion!

With a huge army raised from all parts of his kingdom James moved south into England in the autumn of 1513. On 9 September, he came face to face with a large and powerful English army at Flodden, just over the Border. The battle that followed was an utter disaster for the Scots. The King himself, an archbishop, two bishops, thirteen earls and some ten thousand ordinary soldiers were killed. Almost every family in Scotland lost a relative or friend, and in one terrible day all the promise and achievements of James IV's reign were destroyed.

James V

The new king, James V, was only a baby when James IV died at Flodden, and once again all the old evils associated with regents and over-powerful nobles re-appeared. When he was 16, however, James took over the ruling of the country, and at once began re-asserting the royal power. He established the Court of Session in Edinburgh again, and ruthlessly rooted out the law-breakers. In 1530, he journeyed himself to the Borders, and had the well-known thief, Johnny Armstrong, hanged. The King liked to travel around the country in disguise as 'The Gudeman of Ballangeich', so that he could find out the real conditions of his subjects.

The Reformation

During James V's reign, Scotland was increasingly influenced by the ideas of the Reformation. In 1517, in Germany, Martin Luther denounced the sale of indulgences, and so began the movement which led to the Reformation and the establishment of new Protestant churches outside the Roman Catholic Church. The Reformers placed great emphasis on Bible reading, and printed translations of the Bible and New Testament were soon being carried to many countries, including Scotland.

In Scotland the new ideas met with a favourable reception, for the Church there was in a disgraceful condition. It had become exceedingly wealthy, and many of the bishops and clergy lived luxurious and idle lives. Relatives of the King and the nobles were nominated to important positions regardless of their merits. James IV's son, for example, was made Archbishop of St Andrew's when he was only 11. It was quite common, too, for bishops and other clergy to hold several positions and draw revenues from them all. The ordinary parish priests, on the other hand, were badly paid, and many of them were so illiterate that they could not even carry out the normal services of the Church.

27

Such a Church and such churchmen were naturally hostile to the Reformers, and tried to crush the new movement. They hoped to terrorize the Reformers by arresting Patrick Hamilton, a young scholar who had studied on the Continent and returned to Scotland to preach the new doctrines. In 1528, he was burned as a heretic, but he died so bravely and so courageously that many people were won over to his cause. As one observer put it, 'the reek of master Patrick Hamilton infected as many as it blew upon'.

James V, for his part, was quite determined to support the Roman Catholic Church, and in 1538 he married Mary of Guise, a member of one of the most powerful Catholic families in France. James's policy and his marriage antagonized Henry VIII of England, who in the early 1530s had quarrelled with the Pope and made himself head of the Church in England. In 1542, Henry went to war with France. In order to prevent the Scots from providing assistance to the French, he despatched an army north. The Scots were defeated at the battle of Solway Moss, and two weeks later James V died at Falkland Palace.

16 Mary of Guise, the wife of James V.

James was succeeded by his infant daughter, Mary Queen of Scots. Henry VIII proposed a marriage between his son Edward and the young Mary. When his offer was eventually refused, his armies invaded and devastated large areas of Scotland. This merely made the Scots more determined than ever to resist the English, and the young Queen was sent to France for safety. Mary of Guise became regent, and French troops and advisers were brought over to Scotland to help her rule the country.

17 John Knox reproving the ladies of Queen Mary's Court.

Harsh measures were also taken against the Reformers (or Protestants as they were now being called). In 1546, George Wishart, one of their leaders, was arrested and burned at St Andrews. Nevertheless, the Reformers continued to gain ground, particularly among the nobles and lairds (or small landowners). Many of the nobles hoped that should a revolution occur, they would be able to seize the rich Church lands. In 1557, they joined together in an association known as the Lords of the Congregation to support the Protestants.

Two years later, in 1559, the Reformers found a new spokesman in John Knox. Knox had been a follower of George Wishart, and for some years had been in exile in Geneva. There he had come into contact with the doctrines of the great Reformer, John Calvin, and these were to have a profound effect on later developments in Scotland. Knox was a wonderful orator, and he now began addressing huge crowds throughout the country. His fiery sermons stirred the people up to fever pitch. In Perth, mobs even began looting and plundering the monasteries and abbey there.

By 1559, Scotland was close to revolution. Mary of Guise sent for more French troops to crush the Protestants, but the Protestants then sought assistance from Queen Elizabeth of England. Elizabeth herself had broken with the Catholic Church in 1559, and she had no wish to see French troops in control in Scotland. She therefore sent an English army and fleet to Scotland, and after a short campaign they forced the French to surrender. By the Treaty of Edinburgh (1560), it was agreed that the French should leave Scotland, and that a Scottish Parliament should be summoned to settle the religious question. Mary of Guise had died a short time previously, and thus she did not see the final ruin of her cause, and the end of the 'Auld Alliance' between Scotland and her native France.

The Scottish Parliament met later in 1560, and quickly carried out the Reformation in Scotland. Acts were passed prohibiting the mass and ending the

Pope's authority, while plans and arrangements for the new Church were outlined in a document known as the *First Book of Discipline,* which was drawn up by Knox and others. It also proposed the establishment of a school in every parish throughout the country, and a grammar school in all the important burghs. Unfortunately, not all of these plans were implemented, for the nobles seized much of the Church lands which were to provide the funds for the new arrangements.

Mary Queen of Scots

In 1561, a year after the meeting of the Reformation Parliament, Mary Queen of Scots returned to Scotland. She had been married to Francis II of France, but he had died in 1560. Now, as a Catholic Queen of Protestant Scotland, she faced a tremendously difficult task. Many of the Reformers like Knox disliked her religion and her French ways and manners, and they were always ready to criticise her in public.

18 Mary Queen of Scots.

Nevertheless, Mary made a good start, and in her early years she was popular with the people. She celebrated mass in secret, and declared that she would never attempt to force Catholicism on her subjects. But after she married her cousin Henry Darnley in 1565, her fortunes began to change. Darnley was a strange character. He became so jealous of the Queen's Italian secretary, David Rizzio, that he joined a group of nobles who were conspiring to murder him in Holyrood Palace, in the very presence of the Queen. Soon afterwards Darnley betrayed his fellow conspirators, and in 1567 he himself was murdered. Many people believed that Mary had been involved in his death, but even today the murder of Darnley remains a mystery.

Three months later, Mary married the Earl of Bothwell. Bothwell had been suspected of killing Darnley, and to most people this action seemed to prove that the Queen had been a party to the crime. She lost practically all her

30

19 The murder of David Rizzio.

support, and an army was raised to defeat her. Bothwell fled abroad, and Mary was forced to abdicate in favour of her infant son, born a few months previously. Soon afterwards, she was taken prisoner and locked up in Loch Leven Castle.

Despite all her misfortunes and blunders, Mary could still attract devotion and loyalty. In 1568, a group of conspirators planned her escape, and a young champion named Willie Douglas stole the castle keys and rowed her across the loch to the shore. But this heroic rescue had no happy ending, for the small army which gathered to support her was defeated at Langside near Glasgow. Mary fled to England, and her son was proclaimed King as James VI. Once in England, Mary was immediately imprisoned — Queen Elizabeth feared that the English Catholics might attempt to proclaim her Queen of England. For 19 years she was kept prisoner, and her tragic story ended when the English authorities finally had her executed at Fotheringhay in Northamptonshire.

James VI: union of the crowns

When Mary fled to England, Scotland had once again been left with an infant King. Once again, the nobles set about extending their power and gaining control of the kingdom. In 1587, however, James VI took over control in his own right, and quickly established his authority. The country became relatively peaceful and orderly, and there was a noticeable increase in trade and commerce.

James displayed considerable skill in his handling of the religious situation in the country. The Reformation had established Protestantism, but there were quarrels and disputes about the form the new Church should take. Some wished for a Presbyterian system where the church would be ruled by kirk sessions, presbyteries and a general assembly, while others desired an Episcopalian system with bishops and archbishops. During James's minority, the Presbyterians had had the upper hand, but the King now favoured the Episcopalians. After a few years he managed to re-introduce bishops into the Scottish Church, and although they did not have full powers, they did give support to his own position.

James also achieved some real successes in his relations with England. As Queen Elizabeth grew older, it became evident that she would have no direct heir. As a descendant of Margaret Tudor, James had the strongest claim to the English throne. He therefore strove to maintain friendly relations with Elizabeth, and when eventually she died in 1603, the English authorities invited him south to be King of England.

Social consequences

All these revolutionary developments during the second half of the sixteenth century profoundly affected the lives of ordinary people in Scotland. The Reformers frowned on anything that resembled the medieval church, and attempts were made to ban pilgrimages, feast days and the observance of Christmas, Easter and other festivals. Games, sports and an assorted list of entertainments were forbidden during the Sabbath: 'The Presbytery of Glasgow ordains that if Mungo Craig shall play on his pipes on the Sunday from the sun rising till the sun setting, in any place within the bounds of the Presbytery, that thereafter he shall be summarily excommunicated.'

In these troubled years, too, there was an astonishing outbreak of witchcraft trials, and many unfortunate old women were persecuted, tortured and burned. This strange phenomenon affected all the countries of Western Europe, but in Scotland it was particularly intense. Between 1560 and about 1700, it has been estimated, over 3,500 people were put to death for alleged witchcraft. Sometimes the persecution became so fierce that any old woman who cursed or scolded her neighbours ran grievous risks if they subsequently experienced the slightest misfortune. Many of the victims themselves believed completely in witchcraft, and they often gave vivid descriptions of their cavorting with the Devil and other witches. Here is a confession made by a certain Agnes Sampson in 1590:

32

Upon the night of Allhallow Even, she, with a great many other witches, to the number of 200, went together to sea, each one in a riddle or a sieve; and went with flaggons of wine, making merrie and drinking by the way, to the kirk of North Berwick; and after they had landed, they took hands and danced the reel or short dance.

The history of Scotland during the sixteenth century was not all taken up with religious strife and witchcraft, for during this period there was some continuing advance in the general standard of living. Earlier in the century the kings had begun making improvements to their royal palaces at Holyrood and Linlithgow, and nobles and merchants followed their example by building larger and more comfortable mansions and castles. Trade with France and the Low Countries expanded steadily, and in the second half of the century there were important developments in coal mining and salt manufacturing around the River Forth. By the early seventeenth century, a mine had been cut under the river at Culross in Fife, and people came from far and wide to see this marvel of the age.

20 Holyrood Palace.

The profits made from trade and these new industrial ventures enabled the merchants in the burghs to build fine new stone houses, churches and mansions. At Culross, for example, in the early seventeenth century, the local laird, Sir George Bruce, built a princely palace for himself, and many other stone houses with crow-stepped gables began to appear. In Edinburgh several magnificent mansions were built by powerful merchants and nobles, and the city was rapidly becoming a capital of which the Scots could be proud. Like most towns of the time, it was often haunted with unpleasant smells, and its streets turned into 'a puddle of filth and filthiness'. However, the Englishman

33

21 Linlithgow Palace on its magnificent site above the loch.

Sir William Brereton, who visited the town in 1633, was most impressed by its situation and the six-storeyed buildings that had been erected:

Hence from the Castle you may take a full view of the situation of the whole city, which is built upon a hill nothing oversteep, but sufficiently sloping and ascending to give a graceful ascent to the great street, which I do take to be an English mile long, and is the best paved street with bowther stones (which are very great ones) that I have seen; the channels are very conveniently contrived on both sides the streets, so as there is none in the middle; but it is the broadest, largest and fairest pavement, and that entire, to go, ride or drive upon.

4. One Crown and One Parliament

James VI and I

The accession of James VI of Scotland as King James I of England opened up a new chapter in the tangled history of relations between the two countries. The association was a curious one, for although the two countries had a common monarch, they retained their own separate parliaments and other institutions. James indeed hoped for a complete union, but his English Parliament rejected his proposal. There was so much hostility and jealousy between the two peoples that it was clearly too early for such an idea.

James soon discovered other respects in which his English Parliament could prove stubborn and obstinate. Throughout the sixteenth century it had been growing steadily more powerful, and now on the death of Queen Elizabeth and the arrival of a foreign king, it began increasingly to assert its authority. James therefore found himself at the centre of a fierce struggle, as Parliament

22 Parliament Hall in Edinburgh where the Scottish Parliament met until 1707.

35

criticised his ministers and policies and began limiting the supplies of money granted to him.

In Scotland, on the other hand, James met with much less opposition from the Scottish Parliament. A procedure had been developed whereby representatives from the various estates of clergy, nobles, burgesses and smaller landowners were appointed to a Committee of the Articles to carry on the work of Parliament, and through this Committee the King was able to control Parliament more easily. The Scottish nobles, for their part, had been kept content with grants of land, while the appointing of Wardens on both sides of the Border assisted James in curbing the lawlessness and warfare in that region. Since the Highlands were also relatively quiet, James was able to boast that law and order and his own authority had been established throughout the whole country. 'This I must say for Scotland, here I sit and govern with my pen. I write and it is done, and by a Clerk of the Council I govern Scotland now, which others could not do by the sword.'

But despite all his increased powers in Scotland, James knew full well that his position there could easily be threatened if strife or quarrels broke out once more. He was therefore very careful not to push his subjects too far, and this is perhaps seen most clearly in his religious policies. He continued his attempts to reform the Scottish Church by the Five Articles of Perth (1618) which re-introduced kneeling at Communion, but he avoided measures which would offend the Presbyterians by reminding them too much of Catholic ceremonial and ritual.

National Covenant

James's son, Charles I, however, proved to be much less prudent and statesmanlike when he became king in 1625. He was a rash person, convinced of his own divine right to rule, and he quickly brought himself into serious conflict with his Parliament in England. By 1629, his relations with Parliament had become so bad that he dissolved it and decided to rule without one.

In Scotland, Charles's actions and policies were equally unfortunate. In the first place, he revoked or withdrew all the grants of Church land which had been made to the nobles since 1540. Thus, at one stroke, he alienated this most powerful section of the community. He also antagonized other groups by attempting to bring the Scottish Church into conformity with the Anglican Church in England. A new Prayer Book was drawn up, and Charles ordered that it should be read in all the churches throughout the land.

This was too much for the Scots, and when the new Prayer Book was read for the first time in St Giles's Cathedral in Edinburgh, there was rioting and disorder. In 1638, a committee representing nobles, lairds, burgesses and clergy drew up a National Covenant pledging all who signed it to defend the 'true religion'. Thousands of people throughout the Lowlands signed the document, and soon they were being referred to as the Covenanters. Then, in November 1638, a General Assembly met in Glasgow, where it proceeded to depose the bishops and annul the Prayer Book and the Five Articles of Perth. Charles refused to accept these changes. In 1639 and 1640, he fought two campaigns against the Scots which are now known as the Bishops' Wars. Since the King's army was ill-equipped and only half-trained, however, he was eventually forced to make peace and accept the demands of the Scots.

Civil wars

Charles's difficulties in Scotland forced him to summon his Parliament in England in a vain attempt to obtain supplies. But Parliament was uncooperative, and its relations with the King steadily deteriorated. Finally, in 1642, civil war broke out. In 1643, the Scottish Covenanters entered the war on the side of Parliament in return for an undertaking in the Solemn League and Covenant that Presbyterianism would be introduced into England and Ireland for a minimum period of three years. In 1644, they played a decisive part in the great Parliamentary victory at Marston Moor in Yorkshire. The following year Cromwell, the leader of the Parliamentary forces, inflicted a shattering defeat on the King's army at Naseby, and in 1646 Charles surrendered to his enemies.

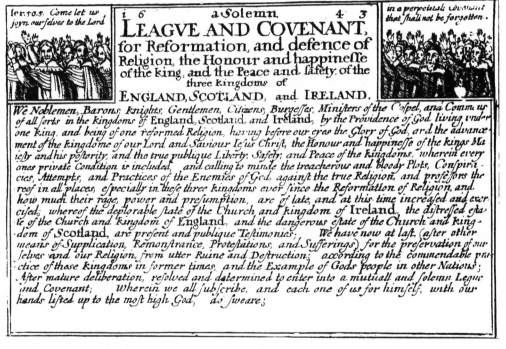

23 Opening section of the Solemn League and Covenant, 1643.

When Parliament refused to introduce Presbyterianism into England, however, the Scots began quarrelling with their former allies. In 1648, they formed an alliance with the Royalists and invaded England, but were overwhelmed by Cromwell at Preston. The King was now brought to trial and executed, and in an outburst of rage the Covenanters proclaimed his son, Charles II, King of Scotland. Cromwell replied in 1650 by invading Scotland and smashing a Scottish army at Dunbar. The following year the Scots invaded England, but

Cromwell pursued them and crushed them at Worcester.

Cromwell now proceeded to consolidate his rule over the British Isles. England, Ireland and Scotland were joined into a Commonwealth with a Parliament at Westminster, but the real power lay with Cromwell as Lord Protector. Law and order were maintained in Scotland by an army of occupation under General Monck, and the country benefited from free trade with England and the English colonies. Nevertheless, the Scots resented losing their independence, and when Cromwell died in 1658 and Charles was restored to the throne in 1660, the majority of the people were glad to see the union ended and Scotland's parliament restored.

Argyll and Montrose

One of the most fascinating and dramatic aspects of those troubled years in Scotland was the rivalry between two great leaders, the Earl of Argyll and the Earl of Montrose. Both men supported the National Covenant and the Bishops' Wars against the King. Later, however, Montrose grew increasingly distrustful of Argyll, who became the dominant political figure amongst the Covenanters. He also opposed the Solemn League and Covenant and decided to support the King in the Civil War. Between 1644 and 1645, Montrose commanded a royal army in the Highlands, but after a series of wonderful victories he was finally defeated at Philiphaugh in 1645. Later, in 1651, he was captured by the Covenanters when leading an expedition in support of Charles II. He was taken to Edinburgh and executed while Argyll looked on in triumph. Argyll was now in an extremely powerful position, but at the Restoration he was tried and executed for treason. Ironically his head was set up on the very same spike in Edinburgh as had been occupied by Montrose's head a short time before.

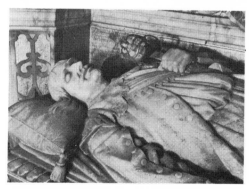 

24 and 25 Memorials to two arch enemies, the Marquis of Argyll (*left*) and the Marquis of Montrose (*right*), both in St Giles Cathedral, Edinburgh.

Persecution of the Covenanters

The execution of Argyll was only one move against the Covenanters, for in the following years the National Covenant was declared illegal and bishops were re-established in the Scottish Church. These changes were resisted by 300 ministers (mainly in the south-west), who were expelled from their parishes. They then began to hold open-air meetings or conventicles, and when these were broken up by the authorities, there were several risings and armed rebellions. The government forces under Graham of Claverhouse were able to suppress these risings, but the authorities were so alarmed that they began a fierce persecution of the Covenanters. This reached a climax in the 'Killing Times' of 1684-85, when some 70 Covenanters were put to death, and hundreds were imprisoned or transported to the colonies.

26 An open-air meeting of the Covenanters.

Revolution of 1688

The persecution of the Covenanters continued during the reign of James VII or II (1685-88), but in 1688 another great revolution in their fortunes occurred. James was a Catholic, and in England he roused great opposition when he began placing Catholics in important positions. This opposition came to a head in 1688, when the birth of his son opened up the prospect of a long line of Catholic kings. In a bloodless revolution, James was replaced by his daughter, Mary, and her husband, William of Orange, acting as joint rulers. A Bill of Rights was then passed limiting the powers of the monarch, and ensuring the rights of the English Parliament.

Scotland, too, accepted William and Mary, although there was some fighting when Claverhouse raised an army for James in the Highlands. He won a victory at Killiecrankie in 1689, but was himself killed in the battle, and soon after his army scattered. In 1690, the Scottish Church finally became Presbyterian, the General Assembly was restored and the bishops deposed. The powers of the Scottish Parliament were also enhanced when the Committee of the Articles was abolished in 1690.

Anglo-Scottish relations

The greater independence of the Scottish Parliament after 1690 made it rather more difficult for William to rule as king of both England and Scotland. The earlier Stuart kings had been able to send their orders north to Scotland and have them obeyed; but now there was a chance that the Scottish Parliament would oppose the king's wishes, and decide to follow policies quite different from those of England.

During the 1690s, too, an increasing number of Scots came to dislike King William, and to find the existing system of having a common king with England quite unsatisfactory. In the Highlands William was extremely unpopular after the Massacre of Glencoe in 1692. The clan chiefs had been ordered to take an oath of loyalty to the new king, but MacIain, the chief of the MacDonalds of Glencoe, was late in taking this oath. The government decided to teach his clan a severe lesson, and a party of troops under Campbell of Glenlyon was sent to the glen. They stayed as guests of the MacDonalds for nearly a fortnight, and then they treacherously attacked and slew nearly 40 men, women and children. William's ministers had signed the orders for this crime, and his government was bitterly condemned for their actions.

Even more Scots were antagonized by the failure of an attempt to establish a Scottish colony at Darien on the Isthmus of Panama. Other European countries had obtained great wealth from colonies, and in 1695 the Scots attempted to follow their example. They raised a huge sum of money, and in 1698 sent out colonists to Darien. Unfortunately the expedition ended in disaster, for the site had been badly chosen, and the Spaniards easily attacked and drove off the colonists. The Scots lost all their money, and they now turned angrily to blame King William and England for the whole fiasco. The English Parliament and East India Company had been opposed to the scheme, and the king had given no support at all to the Scots.

Difficulties in the Scottish economy also helped to create tension between

27 The Act of Union being read before Queen Anne.

England and Scotland. There had been hopes of real economic advance in Scotland in the early years of the seventeenth century and again during the reign of Charles II, but the civil wars and disturbances had blighted these developments. Increasingly, the Scottish economy stagnated, and soon there was not enough work for the whole population. Many Scots were forced to leave their native land, and during the seventeenth century large numbers of them found work as merchants in Poland and Germany, or as soldiers and mercenaries in the armies fighting in the Thirty Years' War (1618-48). At home, the government was compelled to introduce measures to cope with the increasing numbers of poor and unemployed throughout the country, and several laws were passed imposing harsh punishments on vagrants and beggars. By 1672, a Poor Law system had been established whereby each parish had to support its own poor from church collections and incomes from charitable bequests.

Scotland's overseas trade also suffered during the seventeenth century — when England was engaged in wars with France or Holland, Scotland was dragged into the conflict. Since the two countries had the same king, foreign navies and privateers tended to link them together and so treat the Scots as enemies. This meant that by the 1690s, Scotland's trade was overwhelmingly concentrated on the English market. The English government, however, consistently refused to allow the Scots free trade with England or the English colonies. To the Scots, it seemed as if they were having the worst of both worlds — their links with England through the Crown were interfering with trade to Continental countries, but were not bringing any direct benefits in trade with England itself. Not surprisingly, many people were beginning to declare that the situation must be changed. Either Scotland should become independent again with a separate king, or there should be a more complete union between the two countries. Such feelings were further strengthened in the final years of the seventeenth century when a series of bad harvests brought widespread famine and death to many parts of the country.

In this tense and critical situation, the politicians of England and Scotland found themselves faced with the problem of making some new arrangements for the succession. The Revolution Settlement had laid down that Queen Anne would succeed William and Mary, but now it appeared that she would remain childless. In 1701, therefore, the English Parliament passed an Act of Settlement stating that the crown would pass to the Electress of Hanover, a descendant of James VI and I. The English ministers expected the Scottish Parliament to follow suit. Instead, in 1704, the Scots passed an Act of Security proclaiming that they would restore the ancient house of Stewart unless some arrangements were made for giving Scotland access to English and colonial markets.

The situation now moved rapidly towards a crisis. England was at war with France in the War of Spanish Succession, and so was utterly hostile to the prospect of a Stewart king being restored to the Scottish throne, and French influence re-established in Edinburgh. Later, in 1704, tension increased when the Scots passed a Wine Act declaring that they would continue to trade with France. England retaliated in 1705 with an Aliens Act, threatening to treat all

Scots in England as aliens, and to prohibit all trade between the two countries. Armed men and troops began to appear in the Border counties, and it seemed that war might break out at any moment.

Treaty of Union, 1707

The danger of renewed conflict and a return to the situation which had existed before 1603 alarmed moderate men in both England and Scotland, and many of them concluded that the time had come to unite the two countries. Commissioners were appointed by the English and Scottish Parliaments, and they soon discovered that both sides had something to offer and something to gain from a union. The English wished to settle the question of the succession, while the Scots were eager to obtain free trade with England and the English colonies. On this basis, an agreement was drawn up, and in 1707 the proposals

28 Glencoe, the scene of the Massacre.

were passed by both Parliaments.

Under the Treaty of Union, England and Scotland were merged into the new kingdom of Great Britain, and the succession was to pass to the House of Hanover after the death of Queen Anne. There was to be one Parliament and one flag, the English weights and measures were to be adopted in Scotland, and Scotland was to have full and equal trading rights. Scotland, however, was to retain her own law and law-courts, and the Presbyterian Church remained the established church of Scotland.

The Act of Union opened an entirely new phase in the history of Scotland, and offered a new solution to the age-old problem of achieving satisfactory relations with England. But the Union was not at all popular among large sections of the Scottish population, and there were riots in several towns and cities. When it was learned that a sum of money totalling £398,085 had been paid to various people in Scotland, including the shareholders in the Darien Scheme, there were accusations that the Scottish MPs had been bribed. Probably some Scots had indeed been won over by English money, but it could be argued that Union with England at this time was the best solution for the problems then facing Scotland. Her economic prospects were dismal, and entry into the English markets seemed preferable to a return to complete independence, economic decline and possible friction and warfare on the Border.

5. A Century of Fruitful Union, 1707-1832

Results of the Union

Scottish hopes that the Union of 1707 would bring wealth and prosperity were not immediately realized, and indeed some Scottish industries like the woollen industry were adversely affected by competition from the more efficient English enterprises. The imposition of a duty on foreign salt used for curing herring also brought ruin to the east coast fishing industry, while the introduction of English customs and excise duties and officials proved distasteful to the Scots.

From about 1720, however, the benefits of the Union began to work through into the Scottish economy. There was a considerable expansion of the cattle trade, and large numbers of cattle were purchased by English dealers. Even more important was the development of the trade of Glasgow and the Clyde with the West Indies and the American colonies, particularly in tobacco. So successful indeed were the Glasgow merchants that they were able to undercut the tobacco merchants of Bristol and London, and Glasgow soon became a major centre of the tobacco trade in the British Isles.

This great trade from the Clyde was a fascinating enterprise. Many of the Glasgow merchants sent factors to Virginia and other states, and these bought up the crops from the plantation owners. The tobacco was then shipped to the Clyde, from where it could be re-exported to the Continent. The Scottish and English merchants had a complete monopoly, and huge profits could be made as the demand for tobacco increased throughout the countries of Europe. Some of the Glasgow merchants or 'Tobacco Lords' became immensely wealthy, and a stream of wealth poured into the West of Scotland.

The outbreak of the American War of Independence in 1775 ended the British monopoly in the tobacco trade, and many Scottish merchants suffered serious losses. They quickly recovered, however, and developed their trade with the West Indies in sugar, rum and cotton. A reasonable level of trade with the United States was still maintained, but the West Indies now became the main centre for Scottish trade in the later years of the eighteenth century.

From the 1720s, too, there had been considerable developments in the linen industry. In 1727, a body known as the 'Commissioners and Trustees for Improving Fisherys and Manufactures in Scotland' was established, and it began distributing small grants to companies in this field. The industry steadily developed in areas round Glasgow, in Renfrewshire and in Angus. Between 1728 and 1750, the linen cloth stamped for sale increased from 2 million yards to over 7½ million yards.

Assistance was also given to the fishing industry, but at first it produced less satisfactory results. In 1749, however, the government introduced a system of bounties, and during the 1750s and 1760s there was considerable development, particularly on the Clyde where large numbers of vessels began to take part in the herring fishings. Later, in the 1780s, the government bounties and subsidies were increased, and the whole fishing industry was very considerably expanded.

The development of the linen industry and later of the herring fisheries provided Scottish merchants with valuable exports. These helped pay for the imports they obtained from the American colonies and the West Indies, for the plantation owners were eager to obtain the cheap herring and linen cloth for their slave workers. By the end of the century, linen and herring were Scotland's main exports to the West Indies. In the year 1800, over 3½ million yards of linen valued at £187,000, and 34,000 barrels of herring valued at £27,000, were sent out there.

Industrial Revolution

In 1778 important new developments occurred in the textile industry when the first cotton mill in Scotland was built at Penicuik in Midlothian. Some linen

29 Workers in the early cotton manufactures.

mills had been established during the eighteenth century, but it was not until the introduction of water-powered factories at Penicuik, Rothesay, New Lanark and elsewhere that Scotland really began to experience an Industrial Revolution. At first it was only the spinning processes which were mechanized, and an army of hand-loom weavers was employed to supply the mills. But from about 1800 onwards the weaving processes, too, were mechanized, and during the first few decades of the nineteenth century the hand-loom weavers suffered great hardships and unemployment. Steam power was also displacing water power during these years, and it was no longer found necessary to site the mills close to waterfalls and streams. The cotton industry thus came to be centred on Glasgow and the west of Scotland, while the linen industry was concentrated on the east coast in Fife and Angus.

The demand for new machinery helped to stimulate growth in the iron industry in Scotland. Small iron furnaces had been established at Invergarry in 1727 and Taynuilt in 1753 to make use of the abundant Highland timber, but these had not been very successful. Then, in 1759, a coke-using foundry was established at Carron near Grangemouth, and this company soon won considerable business and reputation making guns for the navy. As the Industrial Revolution gathered pace, new foundries were established at Glasgow (the Clyde Works) and in Ayrshire (Muirkirk Company). For some time, the Scottish iron industry lagged behind the English industry. However, when fields of blackband ironstone were discovered in Scotland in 1802, and a new process using a hot-blast furnace was developed in 1828, production costs were slashed and Scottish iron-works began to make rapid progress.

The development of iron furnaces increased the demand for coal, and there was a striking expansion in the Lanarkshire and Ayrshire coalfields. Before 1775, advances were held back by the fact that mineworkers were tied to one particular pit, and were not allowed to leave it to take up employment elsewhere. Miners were bought and sold along with the pits, and sometimes the miners would appear in advertisements listing coalmines for sale. An Act of Parliament in 1775, and another in 1799, finally removed this bondage, but the work underground still remained dangerous and unpleasant.

The expansion of Scottish industry was accompanied and made possible by improvements in transport and communications throughout the country. Canals like the Forth and Clyde Canal (1790) and the Monkland Canal (1792) from Lanarkshire to Glasgow allowed the cheap carriage of coal and other heavy goods; while the improvement of roads and bridges carried out by such engineers as McAdam and Telford speeded up land transport. The Clyde was deepened to allow large ships to sail up river to Glasgow, while many ports and harbours were improved. Early in the nineteenth century steamships were developed, and steamer services were inaugurated on the west coast and between the Clyde and Ireland.

Finance for many of the new industries and other enterprises was provided by the Scottish banking system, which developed and expanded throughout the eighteenth century. The Bank of Scotland (1695), the Royal Bank (1727) and the British Linen Company (1746) were the major institutions, but there were several local banks like the Glasgow Ship Bank (1750) which provided funds

30 *Above* The *Comet*, 1811 – the first successful passenger and freight steamer on the Clyde.

31 *Below* The Royal Bank of Scotland, St Andrews Square, Edinburgh.

for merchants and industrialists. Some individuals who had made a fortune in trade or commerce also invested some of their money directly in new enterprises and industries.

Agricultural Revolution

Scottish farming also underwent profound changes during the eighteenth century. In the early years of the century, the old infield/outfield system which had existed since Norman times still prevailed over most of the country. However, during the 1730s, a few improving landlords such as Sir Archibald Grant of Monymusk (Aberdeenshire) and John Cockburn of Ormiston (East Lothian) set about reorganizing their estates. They enclosed the land into consolidated holdings and gave their tenants longer leases. They introduced new crops such as turnips and potatoes, and also tried to make their land more productive by adopting a system of crop rotation. Later in the century, other landlords followed their example, and the production of food increased rapidly. The countryside was quite transformed, and by 1800 Scottish farmers were themselves beginning to pioneer new methods and approaches. In the early nineteenth century, for example, two Scottish farmers, Hugh Watson and William McCombie, developed the Aberdeen-Angus cattle, one of the world's finest breeds of beef cattle.

Population and society

The changes in Scottish agriculture and industry were accompanied by a remarkable increase in the country's population during the second half of the

32 Polled Angus bulls at an Agricultural show in 1884.

33 Glasgow about 1828.

eighteenth century. According to an enumeration conducted by a minister, the
Rev Alexander Webster, the population of Scotland in 1755 stood at
1,265,000; by the first national census of 1801, this had risen to 1,608,000.
There were steady increases registered over the succeeding decades – 1,806,000
in 1811, 2,092,000 in 1821, 2,364,000 in 1831. There was also a considerable
re-distribution of the population as people from the Highlands and other rural
areas of Scotland moved into the expanding industrial towns such as Glasgow,
Paisley, Greenock, Dumbarton and Motherwell. By the early nineteenth
century, too, a large number of migrants from Ireland were beginning to arrive
in the West of Scotland, and these newcomers helped to swell the growing
population.

This dramatic increase in Scotland's population was probably a result of
both an increase in the birth rate and a decline in the death rate. Young men
and women employed in the new factories may have married earlier, while the
demand for children in the textile mills may have helped produce an increase in
the size of families. The development of hospitals, the improvement in diet and
medical care, and the introduction of inoculation and later of vaccination
against smallpox would also have helped to reduce the death rate. It was
calculated that, in the 1780s, about one-fifth of all children born alive died of
smallpox before they were 10. With the growing acceptance of vaccination
after 1796, thousands upon thousands of young lives were saved.

Changes in the structure of the Scottish population also occurred around this time. In Glasgow and other commercial and industrial centres a new prosperous middle class appeared, whose members began building fine mansions in specially selected areas of their towns. Alongside this development a new working class was also being formed among the labourers and craftsmen in the factories and new industries. At first they had little coherence as a group. However, by the early years of the nineteenth century, they were developing a self-conscious awareness of their identity and common interests, and were already referring to themselves as the working class.

Politics

The tremendous changes in the economy and social structure gradually influenced the political system of the country. In 1707, Scotland had been allotted 45 MPs in the House of Commons, and 16 peers in the House of Lords. Initially, the electorate was a very small one. In the burghs, the town council or a small group of ruling merchants normally controlled the elections, while in the country districts only a small group of landowners possessed the freehold land that entitled them to vote.

The small electorate made it relatively easy for powerful politicians to control elections. By the middle of the eighteenth century, the Duke of Argyll was able to manage the system and to 'appoint' a majority of the Scottish MPs. In the 1780s, this role was taken over by Robert Melville, Lord Dundas. In the years that followed, he came to control the majority of the Scottish parliamentary seats. Dundas was a director of the East India Company, and he used the enormous patronage this gave him to establish his authority. Voters in elections could obtain a position for a friend or relative if they supported Dundas's candidate, and in this way a steady stream of Scots poured into the service of the East India Company.

Many people in Scotland were dissatisfied with this system. After the French Revolution of 1789, several societies were set up which demanded the reform of Parliament. The government was afraid of a revolution in Britain, however. It passed severe laws against the reformers, and imposed harsh sentences on their leaders. Such measures helped keep the situation relatively quiet throughout the French Wars until 1815, but thereafter the government increasingly feared a rising. In 1820, a few weavers did actually march from Glasgow to seize the Carron Iron Works, but they were easily dispersed by cavalry.

Gradually the government's hostility to change was diminished during the 1820s, as more and more people began to press for parliamentary reform. The new emerging middle classes, for their part, felt that their improved economic status entitled them to some voice in the running of the country. Similar demands were being made throughout the United Kingdom. In 1832, Parliament passed the Reform Act which extended the franchise to the middle classes, and gave Scotland an additional eight MPs.

Religion and culture

Important changes were also taking place in the religious life of Scotland during this period. Throughout the eighteenth century the Church of Scotland

51

52   **34** The Scottish poet Robert Burns, 1759-96.

remained in a dominant position, but there were several internal quarrels which led to splinter groups seceding and setting up separate Presbyterian churches. Within the Church of Scotland, the more fiery zeal of the seventeenth-century Covenanters diminished, and control passed to the Moderates, a group of churchmen who placed much more emphasis on general culture, and who were even prepared to visit the theatre or play cards! Among the new emerging working classes in the industrial towns, too, there was a decline in religious enthusiasm. Many of them ceased attending church altogether. In the early nineteenth century, an additional element was added to the religious scene when the arrival of hundreds of immigrants from Ireland meant that the Catholic Church was re-established in the industrial towns of the west of Scotland.

The general cultural life of Scotland was also being changed and transformed during the eighteenth century. Many Scottish authors began writing in English, and the upper classes ceased to speak Scots and instead used English. They even founded a Select Society in Edinburgh in 1761 so that they might remove 'the barbaric Scots sounds' from their speech. An increasing number of Scottish writers and artists, too, left Scotland to live in London, where there was a much larger market and greater opportunities for them.

In the late eighteenth century, however, there was a remarkable flourishing of Scottish culture. In Edinburgh, for example, such a galaxy of writers

35 A view of Edinburgh's New Town, with Charlotte Square in the centre.

emerged in various fields that this has been called the city's 'Golden Age'. Thus Hume in philosophy, Burns with his poetry, Home in drama, Adam Smith in political economy, Scott with his novels and numerous others produced works of such quality that the proud citizens began claiming that Edinburgh was the 'Athens of the North'.

In appearance, too, Edinburgh soon came to be worthy of such a title. The old town built on the castle ridge had become grossly overcrowded. Starting in 1767, a New Town designed by the architect James Craig was built across the Nor Loch. With broad streets like George Street and elegant squares like Charlotte Square, the New Town became one of the most famous examples of town planning in the world. Even today, countless thousands of visitors come to Edinburgh to study and admire it.

Conclusion

In the hundred years since the Act of Union in 1707, a new Scotland had emerged. From a poor, underdeveloped country, she had been transformed into one of the leading industrial countries in the world. Scotland and Scotsmen were making important contributions in many different fields. Most Scots accepted that all this had been made possible by the Act of Union, and increasingly they were satisfied with and proud of their role in the United Kingdom.

Pride in the United Kingdom was intensified by the part Scots had played in creating an enlarged British Empire in Canada, the West Indies and India during the eighteenth century. Scottish soldiers and regiments had served in the wars against France, while Scottish merchants and settlers had been prominent in opening up new areas. A climax was reached during the French Revolutionary and Napoleonic Wars (1793-1815) — the British triumphs in that conflict created a real sense of a British identity in Scotland. The Union clearly seemed a success story, and many leading Scots in this period took to calling themselves North Britons and their country North Britain.

6. The Other Scotland: The Highlands

Highland society

Although Scotland as a whole had quite certainly prospered in the century after the Act of Union, the Highlands had not shared in the general economic and industrial advance. For centuries, this great area of Scotland lying beyond the Highland Line had had a distinctive way of life, and during the eighteenth century it responded differently to the tremendous changes taking place throughout the country. However, what was happening in the Highlands was of great importance to Scotland as a whole, and events in the north seriously affected the country's general development.

The Highlands had always presented a problem to the kings of Scotland. Although James IV and James VI had achieved some success there, they had not managed to bring the area permanently under their control. At that time it was impossible to maintain effective royal power in such a remote and mountainous region, and instead the kings concentrated on cutting down the powers of dangerous chiefs and setting up more loyal chieftains in their stead. Both James IV and James VI, for instance, took steps to curb the power of the

36 A Highland loch — Loch Maree in Ross-shire. Such terrain was difficult for the authorities to control.

MacDonalds, and to advance the Campbells under their chief, the Earl of Argyll, to prominence.

Highland society was organized on a military basis, and the clans could be quickly mobilized to follow their chiefs to war. The chief let out lands to prominent clansmen known as tacksmen, and they in turn rented out small townships or clachans to groups of ordinary clansmen. On these the Highlanders raised a few cereal crops and the small black cattle that were the basis of the Highland economy. When they wished to increase their herds, they would raid their neighbours or the Lowlands. On such raids and in time of war, the tacksmen (who leased land and in turn sublet it) acted as the officers of the clan forces — they would bring out their tenants to the clan muster.

By the early seventeenth century, there were signs of increasing tension and hostility between the Highlanders and the Lowlanders. The Highlanders' way of life with its distinctive style of dress, its bagpipes, and its Gaelic language and civilization seemed utterly alien to the Lowlanders, while their repeated raids to steal cattle aroused anger and resentment. The Reformation had added to these differences, for difficulties of communication had prevented the Reformed Church from sending clergymen to all areas of the Highlands. In the lands of the Campbells in Argyll, Presbyterianism did make some real headway, but in many areas the Highlanders favoured Episcopalianism, while in a few districts like Barra, Lochaber and parts of Banffshire the Roman Catholic Church retained its position. This meant that the National Covenant was not received with equal enthusiasm throughout the Highlands. The Marquis of Argyll and his clansmen gave it their support, but this in itself was sufficient to drive many of the clans to the opposite side. The growth of Campbell power had roused much jealousy and enmity among the MacDonalds and other clans, and they were ready and eager to fight against them.

Montrose

This was the situation in the Highlands in 1644, when the Marquis of Montrose was given a commission by Charles I to raise a royal army in the north. Montrose raised the royal standard at Blair Atholl, and there he was joined by the Stewarts, Robertsons and other clans, as well as by a small detachment of MacDonalds from Ireland. From Blair Atholl, Montrose marched towards Perth. At Tippermuir, a few miles from the city, he encountered a much larger and better equipped Covenanter army.

Although they were greatly outnumbered, the Highlanders swept forward in a furious charge. The Covenanters had time to fire only a few scattered shots from their artillery before the clansmen were upon them. The Covenanters were carrying pikes, but it soon became evident that they were no match at close quarters for the Highlanders. As the Lowland soldier lunged clumsily forward with his pike, his blow would be easily parried by the clansman's shield. Then with a fierce swing the Highlander's claymore (or big sword) would come crashing down on the unprotected head of the unfortunate Covenanter. Soon the army of the Covenanters broke in terror and fled back to Perth.

For over a century after Tippermuir, this terrible Highland charge was to prove a well nigh invincible weapon, and many an English and Lowland army fled in panic before it. Montrose, however, soon discovered the weaknesses of a Highland army. In 1645, he won great victories at Inverlochy, Auldearn and Kilsyth, but after each battle more of his men would disappear home with their booty. The clansmen were also reluctant to leave the Highlands and follow Montrose to England, and his weakened army was defeated at Philiphaugh near Selkirk by the Covenanters' army returning from England.

The Jacobites

During the following century, the Highland clans continued to play a significant part in national affairs. After the Revolution of 1688, for example, many of the clans remained loyal to James VII, and the rebellion of Claverhouse and the massacre at Glencoe were important consequences of that loyalty. Those who continued to support James VII were known as Jacobites, after *Jacobus,* the Latin word for James, but once again the Highlands were divided. Clan Campbell supported the new rulers, William and Mary, and after 1714 the Hanoverian George I. But the MacDonalds, Stewarts, Camerons and others continued to look favourably on the old House of Stewart. In 1715, many of the clans joined a Jacobite rebellion which hoped to place the Old Pretender, the son of James VII, on the throne. The rising was badly organized, however, and when the English Jacobites were crushed at Preston, and the advance of the Highland army was held at Sheriffmuir by the Duke of Argyll, it collapsed in defeat.

Thirty years later, in 1745, a much more dangerous rising occurred when Prince Charles, the son of the Old Pretender, landed at Moidart in Inverness-

37 Battle of Culloden.

shire. He was accompanied by only seven companions, but once again many of the clans flocked to his standard. This time the Jacobites gained control of Scotland and advanced as far south as Derby. But there they decided to retreat, and in April, 1746, the rebellion was finally crushed at Culloden near Inverness.

At Culloden, an answer was at last found to the dreaded Highland charge. Government artillery and grapeshot took a terrible toll of the Highlanders, and the government infantry had been taught new tactics for hand-to-hand fighting. Each man in the front rank was trained to lunge forward with his bayonet, not towards the clansman immediately in front of him, but to the man on his right. This Highlander would have his arm uplifted to strike with his claymore, and thus would have no defence against the bayonet thrust. In this way the government lines were able to withstand the shock of the Highland charge and throw the clansmen back.

End of the clan system

Nevertheless the achievements of the Jacobite clans had been spectacular. Only about 5,000 clansmen out of a potential Highland force of about 20,000 actually joined the rebellion, and without doubt a united Highland army could easily have swept to victory. The British authorities had been extremely alarmed, and now they proceeded to remove this threat from the Highlands once and for all. Wounded Jacobites lying on Culloden Moor were ruthlessly bayoneted, rebel chiefs and ordinary clansmen were executed or transported to the colonies, and an army of occupation spread fire and terror among the glens. Houses where rebels had sheltered were destroyed, while the cattle on which the people and the whole clan economy depended were driven off by government troops.

The government also introduced measures to destroy the whole pattern of life and society in the Highlands. The estates of those chiefs who had taken part in the rebellion were forfeited and administered by men prepared to adopt and introduce new ideas. All Highland chiefs lost their special powers of jurisdiction over their clansmen, while laws were passed forbidding the wearing of the kilt, the playing of bagpipes, and the carrying and possession of arms by Highlanders.

The defeat at Culloden and the subsequent acts of the government did much to bring the clan system to an end. But already, before 1746, important changes had been taking place in certain areas, particularly in southern Argyll. Where in earlier times a chief's main aim had been to keep as many clansmen on his lands as possible, he now became much more interested in obtaining profits from his estates. Many of the tacksmen lost their lands, for the chiefs could obtain larger rents by letting the land directly to the tenants. In some instances, indeed, chiefs and landlords were prepared to rent land to tenants from the Lowlands who could farm it more efficiently and with greater returns. In these ways, the traditional bonds of the clan system were weakened, and the ties of loyalty between the chiefs and their clansmen were loosened.

The Highland economy

Many of the Highland chiefs and landlords also tried to encourage commercial and industrial development on their estates, and the second half of the eighteenth century saw some economic advance in the Highlands. The cattle trade was expanded, some iron furnaces were founded to make use of Highland timber, a few cotton factories were established near the Highlands, and the fishing industry experienced considerable growth. Most dramatic of all, perhaps, was the development of the kelp industry where kelp was processed from seaweed — many landlords on the west coast and islands made large profits from this. But there was no large-scale development of commerce and industry in the Highland area to compare with what was happening in the Lowlands at the time, and the Highlands remained largely rural and agricultural.

38 Highlanders gathering and burning kelp.

As in the Lowlands, the population of the Highlands was rising steadily during the final decades of the eighteenth century. However, since there were no large towns or industries to provide employment for them, great numbers were forced to leave their homes. The breaking of the clan ties and loyalties made it easier for the Highlanders to move to other areas. During the late eighteenth and nineteenth centuries, many thousands of people moved south to the growing towns of the Lowlands, or emigrated to new lands in Canada, America and Australia. Once there they wrote letters home urging their friends

59

39 Emigrants leaving for America.

and relatives to join them. Here is such a letter written from Australia in the nineteenth century:

Dear John,

It grieves me very much the value that this new Proprietor, the Duke of Leeds, puts on his land, and I think it is a thing impossible for his tenants to meet. I do firmly believe, John, if your Father and Mother was to end their days in peace in their ancient place of abode it would be advisable for you to shift your quarters to this place where the Duke of Leeds cannot rise the rent. You may make yourself sure whatever branch of labour that you will feel yourself inclined to put your hand to clear from £40 to £50 a year.

Clearances and depression

Although many Highlanders left their homes willingly to seek a better life in other places, a large number were dispossessed by chiefs or landlords to make way for great herds of sheep. In the 1820s, for example, the Duke and Duchess of Sutherland were particularly active in clearing their lands in Sutherland, and

40 An old Highland dwelling.

the homes of hundreds of tenants were burned down. In other parts of the Highlands, some chiefs even went so far as to drive their people aboard an emigrant-ship which would take them away to Canada.

Conditions in the Highlands during the early decades of the nineteenth century were made worse by a general economic decline in the area. The ending of the Napoleonic Wars in 1815 brought foreign competition and ruin to the kelp industry, and with other activities like fishing and the cattle trade suffering setbacks, the outlook was bleak. In the 1830s and 1840s, there were also severe food shortages and famine as the potato crops failed. As in Ireland the potato had become the basic food of many Highlanders, and now there was mass suffering and destitution.

Up until about 1840, the population of the Highlands had continued to rise despite all the migration from the area; but now the disasters of these years led to a new massive movement of people away from the region and a considerable drop in population in many districts. In some areas, this trend was intensified as landlords began replacing sheep with herds of deer, for even fewer workers were required to tend them. All this set in motion a vicious process whereby

41 Cheviot sheep on the heather moors of Sutherland.

the population in certain districts became so low that the communities proved less and less attractive to the younger people and could provide no employment for them. Clachans, hamlets and homesteads were deserted, and thus was consolidated that depopulation of the Highlands that has made the area a problem right down to modern times.

Highland culture
The tremendous disruptions affecting the economy and society of the Highlanders during the nineteenth century produced many changes in their whole way of life. In the early years of the century, for example, there were great religious revivals in many districts. Large numbers of people turned away from

42 Deer hunting in the Highlands.

he miseries of their lives to adopt an extreme form of Presbyterianism which laid great stress on a strict Sabbath observance. The Gaelic language was adversely affected as education in English was imposed in the schools, and in many areas the people ceased to speak the old language. It seemed that their spirit had been wrenched out of the Highland people, and that the Highland language, culture and traditions were being steadily eroded.

And yet strangely enough, even as the Highland culture and civilization seemed to be on the defensive in its homelands, things Highland were gaining in increased popularity in Lowland Scotland. Sir Walter Scott in his novels had romanticized the Highlands, and the deeds of the Highland regiments in the wars against France had gained them a tremendous reputation. Throughout the nineteenth century, too, more and more people were coming to appreciate wild and rugged scenery, and a multitude of tourists flocked north to enjoy the splendours of the Highland mountains and lochs. These tourists were often shocked by the deserted hamlets and homesteads, and steadily there was a growing demand that evictions and clearances in the Highlands should be halted. In response to public pressure, the government set up a Royal Commission (the Napier Commission) to investigate the whole question of land-holding in the Highlands. Its report was issued in 1884.

The evidence placed before the Napier Commission told a sorry tale of evictions and selfish actions on the part of the Highland landlords. The commissioners were completely convinced that more protection should be given to the Highland tenants, and to implement their recommendations the government passed the Crofters' Act of 1886. This gave security of tenure and fixed rents to small Highland tenants, and set up a Crofters' Commission with powers to supervise the crofting lands. It was hoped that the crofters in their small-holdings would be able to find part-time employment as fishermen, foresters or roadmen, and that this and their land would provide them with an income large enough to keep them in the Highlands.

43 Loch Duich and the Five Sisters of Kintail, Ross and Cromarty.

7. Boom and Expansion in the Nineteenth Century

The economy

While the Highlands were suffering economic decline and distress for much of the nineteenth century, the industrial Lowlands and other parts of the country continued to prosper. By the middle of the century, Britain had become the leading industrial power, 'the workshop of the world', and Scottish industries played their part in winning this reputation. The cotton industry did begin to decline from the 1830s, but this setback was more than made good by a dramatic expansion in the iron industry, now mainly centred around Glasgow and Lanarkshire. Between 1835 and 1869, for instance, the annual output increased from 75,000 tons to 1.15 million tons, and Scottish iron products were exported to many countries overseas. In the second half of the century, too, Scotland developed a flourishing steel industry that kept her in the forefront of economic and technological advance.

Other prosperous areas of the Scottish economy in this period were the shipbuilding and marine engineering industries of the Clyde. Ships had been built at Scott's of Greenock from 1711, but it was only in the early nineteenth century that large-scale developments took place. Some of the first steamships were built there, and later in the century Clyde shipyards were among the

44 The *Majestic*, built by Scott's of Greenock in 1820. This is the oldest portrait of a sea-going steamer in existence.

pioneers producing iron-hulled and steel ships. Clydeside marine engineering firms were also active in developing improved steam engines and steam turbine engines, and they quickly won a world-wide reputation. Production increased steadily throughout the century, and in 1913 a record tonnage of some 756,976 tons was launched on the Clyde.

As the Clyde became famous as a shipbuilding river, her engineers and other craftsmen gained world-wide renown. Boys were eager to serve an apprenticeship there, for they would receive a thorough training in all the latest engines and processes of the day. When a youth had completed his apprenticeship on the Clyde, he might go to sea as an engineer with one of the great Scottish shipping companies like the Allan, Donaldson or Anchor Lines. After some years, he might even become a chief engineer, and one of that legendary band of craftsmen who carried their skills and their fame to every corner of the globe. Even today, the Scottish engineer is a favourite character among writers and dramatists, and no ship ever sails in book, play or on the screen without his being there to service the engines.

On land during this period, a new system of rail transport was developed in Scotland. Early railways for carrying goods appeared in the 1820s, and in the 1840s there was a great burst of railway-building activity. The Glasgow-Greenock line was opened in 1841, the Glasgow-Edinburgh in 1842, and Edinburgh to Berwick and England in 1846. Over the next few decades a network of lines covering the whole country was completed by the great Scottish railway companies — the North British, the Caledonian, the Glasgow and South Western, the Highland, the Great North of Scotland. Railway engines for these companies were built at locomotive engineering works in Glasgow and other centres. Later as other countries came to develop railway systems, Scottish engines were exported to many parts of the world.

Interesting developments also occurred in finance and banking during the nineteenth century. Perhaps the most successful of these were the investment trusts where individuals invested their money in a trust and it was then channelled into a wide range of companies and activities. The money was skilfully managed, and large sums were invested in profitable foreign undertakings. Some three-quarters of the foreign money invested in American ranching in the 1880s, for example, came from Scotland, and such investments brought back substantial returns to Scottish investors. It is worth remembering, though, that money which could have encouraged further development in Scotland itself was thus being diverted to foreign lands.

Scottish farming, on the other hand, had rather mixed fortunes during the nineteenth century. From 1815 onwards, agriculture was protected by the Corn Laws which placed import duties on foreign corn. The repeal of these Laws in 1846 did not immediately damage the farming interests. The farmers enjoyed a steady and growing prosperity, and the years around the middle of the century became known as a 'Golden Age'. Here, for example, is a description of a prosperous farm in East Lothian in the 1860s:

A fine new farmhouse of red sandstone had recently been built and the old homestead handed over to the steward. It stood on a broad ridge commanding a considerable slice of East Lothian, and much more besides. For miles in nearly all directions there were great sweeps of tillage patterned in large rectangular fields, the hedgerows, short and trimmed like garden fences, showing as mere straight lines. The land was as clean as a well-kept garden, and the whole farm subsoil drained with tile pipes. Red roofed steadings, planted at intervals about the land, shot tall brick chimneys skyward, some of them a-smoke in evidence that thrashing was going forward. For every farm had its fixed engines and machinery and its own steam-plough.

From about 1875, however, this cheerful picture changed as cheap wheat began pouring in from the American Middle West to undercut Scottish farmers. A few years later, the development of refrigerated ships made possible the transport of cheaper meat from Australia and America, and beef producers suffered fierce competition. Dairy produce from Holland and Denmark was also cheaper than anything Scottish farmers could provide. The combination of these factors brought about a serious depression in Scottish farming during the 1880s and 1890s. Milk producers in Ayrshire and prime beef producers in the north-east continued to do well, but many other farmers suffered severe hardships. There was some improvement in the early years of the twentieth century, but right up until 1914 and the beginning of the First World War, Scottish farmers experienced difficult times.

Farm workers, for their part, had much more cause to complain than the farmers. Their wages were barely at subsistence level. On large farms, single men were housed in bothies or hostels where conditions were often deplorable:

As a general rule the bothy consists of a portion of the farm buildings or steading formed into a single room of moderate size. It is supplied with no

45 A Sutherland township at Skerray.

separate sleeping compartments, and nobody is employed to clean it or to make the beds; a heap of coals will be seen in one corner and of firewood in another; it is furnished with no tables and no seats, so that on returning from work the only place which the servants have to sit down upon is their chests. The bothies are but rarely ventilated. In a few cases I have met with bothies attached to the stables where the ventilation (if indeed it can be so called) was of the worst description.

The difficulties facing Scottish farming towards the end of the nineteenth century intensified the movement of people away from country districts into the towns. Between 1851 and 1891, the proportion of country dwellers fell from about two-thirds of the population to about one-third. The numbers of town and city dwellers rose steadily. By 1900 Glasgow's population was 916,000, Edinburgh's 402,000, Dundee's 171,000, and Aberdeen's 153,000.

During the nineteenth century, too, the Irish element in the population of Glasgow and other towns in west-central Scotland became a significant one. In 1861, for example, some 7 per cent of the population of Scotland had been born in Ireland, while about 15 per cent of the population of Glasgow were Irish. These migrants took up a wide range of occupations. Many of them joined the gangs of workers and navvies who helped build the railways, harbours, docks, reservoirs and other public works throughout Scotland during this period.

The navvies were a fascinating body of men, but they were often regarded as rowdy hooligans by the inhabitants of the area in which they were working. They could earn high wages by toiling long hours, but too often the money was spent on gambling and wild drinking. The navvies were usually proud of their notorious reputation, and one of them wrote about their failings and short-

46 Building the Forth (Railway) Bridge.

comings in an amusing and beautifully descriptive poem:

> We of the soapless legion, we of the hammer and hod.
> Human swine of the muck pile, forever forgotten of God.

Nevertheless, it was men like these who transformed the face of Scotland. With their shovels, picks and bare hands, they created the structure and the materials of our modern industrial society.

Social conditions

The towns and cities of Lowland Scotland were soon flooded with people from Ireland, and also from the Highlands and other rural districts. This created many serious social problems. The wealthy merchants and industrialists were able to build fine mansions for themselves, but the ordinary people were crowded into one- or two-roomed tenement houses with no proper toilet facilities. Some attempts were made to provide better accommodation in the second half of the nineteenth century, but conditions remained grim right through until the beginning of the twentieth century.

47 A row of old houses in a Scottish village. Lavatories are shown by the projecting sections, and communal wash houses are situated at the end of the row.

In the early part of the nineteenth century, too, the sanitary conditions in most of the towns and cities were appalling. There was no proper drainage system, and often the sewage was thrown into the streets, and left to seep into the water supplies. Just how loathsome and foul-smelling the streets could become is vividly illustrated by a description of Greenock in Renfrewshire as it appeared in 1842:

> In one part of Market Street is a dunghill — yet it is too large to be called a dunghill. I do not misstate its size when I say it contains 100 cubic yards of impure filth. This collection is fronting the public street; it is enclosed in front by a wall; the height of the wall is almost 12 feet, and the dung overtops it; the malarious moisture oozes through the wall, and runs over the pavement.
>
> The effluvia all round this place in summer is horrible. There is a tenement adjoining, and in the summer each house swarms with myriads of flies; every article of food and drink must be covered, otherwise the flies immediately attack it, and it is rendered unfit for use, from the strong taste of the dunghill left by the flies.

Not surprisingly, there were frequent epidemics in these early industrial towns. In the 1830s, for example, there was a widespread cholera epidemic, while in the 1850s and 1860s there were serious outbreaks of typhus. Initially, the more prosperous citizens in Scotland blamed the habits of the poorer people for these outbreaks, but when the epidemics affected their own areas they began to insist that controls of some sort should be imposed. Because of this pressure, several Public Health Acts were passed, during the second half of the century, which led to local authorities providing proper water supplies and installing drainage and sewage systems. Medical officers were also appointed to carry out inspections, and they were given powers to place people suffering from infectious and contagious diseases in quarantine. All these measures helped to improve the situation, and by the end of the century typhus and cholera had been practically eradicated.

Attempts were also made during the nineteenth century to improve conditions of work. In the early part of the century men had laboured long hours in atrocious conditions in return for low wages, but succeeding governments and the growing power of the trade unions had steadily reduced hours of work and improved wages and conditions. Some measures were also introduced to assist the poor and sick. Before the nineteenth century, the parish had supported its poor with funds obtained from church collections. In 1845, a Poor Law Amendment Act was passed transferring control from church to lay authorities. Nevertheless, the funds applied to helping the poor were still extremely small, and often the destitute were forced to enter grim and dismal workhouses. In the first decade of the twentieth century, however, the government introduced Old Age Pensions and National Health Insurance and Unemployment Insurance for some groups of workers, and a first step had been taken towards creating a welfare state.

Scottish society

In many other ways, too, the lives of the people of Scotland were improved during this period. The building of railways and the development of steamship services made travel much easier and cheaper, and enabled thousands of people

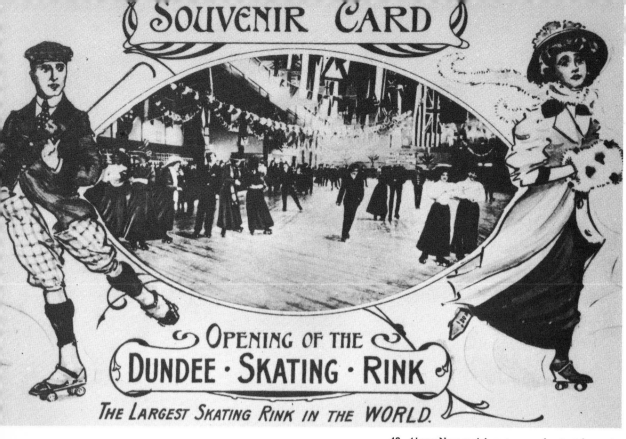

SOUVENIR CARD

OPENING OF THE DUNDEE · SKATING · RINK

THE LARGEST SKATING RINK IN THE WORLD.

48 *Above* New social customs and entertainments.

49 *Below* Portobello Beach, 1910.

to enjoy holidays at the Clyde resorts, in the Highlands and elsewhere. In the towns and cities, theatres became increasingly popular, while later in the century music halls attracted large audiences. Many people were interested in sport, and after the first soccer international between Scotland and England in 1872, increasingly large crowds were drawn to football matches. Towards the end of the century, the more active began taking jaunts into the countryside on the new-fangled bicycles, while from the 1890s onwards, the rich could venture out on the first expensive and temperamental motor cars.

Scotland's educational system also underwent considerable changes during the nineteenth century. Before the Industrial Revolution the country had a relatively efficient system with schools in almost every parish, grammar schools in the burghs, and a real opportunity for even a poor youth to go on to university at St Andrews, Glasgow, Aberdeen or Edinburgh. But the rapid growth of the population in the industrial towns overloaded the existing structure, and in 1872 an Act of Parliament established a state system of education. Elected school boards in local areas were set up to provide a primary education to equip pupils for the new industrial society. Shortly afterwards, education was made compulsory. In the early years of the twentieth century, an increasing number of secondary schools providing for more advanced education were also established.

Although the Church of Scotland had now given up its control of education, it still continued to play an important part in the life of the country. This was despite the fact that it had suffered the 'Great Disruption' in 1843, when 400 ministers and large numbers of their congregations had left to set up the Free Church of Scotland. They were opposed to the practice of a local landlord appointing the minister of a parish church. In their new Church, they made sure that each congregation elected its own minister.

Politics

Throughout the nineteenth century, there were important developments on the Scottish political scene. The Reform Act of 1832 had brought Scotland firmly within the parliamentary structure of the United Kingdom, and increasingly Scotland participated in the various movements affecting other parts of the country. Thus there were Chartists in Scotland in the 1840s asking for an extension of the franchise, and suffragettes in the early twentieth century demanding votes for women. Scotland also shared in the extension of the franchise. The Reform Act of 1867 gave the vote to the working classes in the towns, the Act of 1884 gave it to the agricultural workers, that of 1918 to women over 30, and another of 1928 to all men and women over 21.

The political parties in Scotland were also similar to those in the United Kingdom as a whole. The Whigs and Tories were the major parties in the early part of the century, and the Liberals and Conservatives in the later years. A Labour Party emerged in Scotland during the early years of the twentieth century, and Scottish politicians like Keir Hardie played a prominent part in the emergence of a similar party in England. But there were certain features of the political scene that were peculiar to Scotland, for the Liberal Party there tended to be much more dominant than its counterpart in England. Liberals

72

and Conservatives tended to alternate as governments of the United Kingdom, but in Scotland the Liberals were almost always the majority party. During the 1880s, too, the separate nature of certain Scottish problems was recognized. A Scottish Secretary and a Scottish Office were established with responsibility for large areas of government in Scotland.

This movement towards a separate Scottish administrative system did not, however, indicate any real discontentment with the existing constitutional arrangements. The United Kingdom appeared to be more successful and more powerful than ever — the British Navy ruled the oceans of the world, and vast new territories and colonies in Africa and Asia were added to the Empire during the nineteenth century. So, as they moved into the twentieth century, the vast majority of Scotsmen still accepted uncritically their role and position in this great enterprise, and assumed that the triumphs and achievements of Britain and her Empire would be maintained and perhaps even surpassed in the future.

50 *Opposite* Keir Hardie (1856-1915), the radical Scottish politician who founded the Independent Labour Party, and worked hard towards the ideal of a socialist state.

8. Wars and Depression

The First World War

Despite the apparent strength and supremacy of Britain and the British Empire in 1900, her power and position were already being seriously challenged. Germany in particular was emerging as a potential danger. After her unification by Bismarck in 1871, she had become the strongest power on the Continent. Towards the end of the nineteenth century, she began building a large navy with the intention of rivalling British sea power, and the centuries-old British command of the seas was threatened.

During the first decade of the twentieth century, fear of Germany's growing military and naval strength brought Britain closer to her old rivals, France and Russia. Europe had been divided into two great opposing alliances, with Germany, Austria and Italy on one side, and France and Russia on the other. As one international crisis followed another, so tension mounted. In 1914, a great European war was finally sparked off by the assassination of an Austrian Archduke. One after the other the Great Powers were dragged in. When Germany invaded Belgium, Britain entered the conflict — she had guaranteed Belgian neutrality in the 1830s, and was alarmed at the prospect of Germany controlling the Channel coastline opposite England.

The First World War (1914-18) was one of the most terrible conflicts in the history of Europe. All the countries involved raised huge armies, and then suffered enormous casualties as they engaged in savage and costly trench warfare. Britain raised large armies and naval forces, who were joined by powerful units from Australia, New Zealand, South Africa, Canada, India and other parts of the Empire. It seemed as if Britain's great world-wide Empire had become a living reality, which could attract the loyalty and devotion of countless millions of people throughout the world.

Scotland's part in the struggle was an important one. Her shipyards and factories poured out warships, merchant ships, guns, armaments and other war materials. Once again, too, the Scottish regiments fought with distinction on all the major battlefields. Something of the old glory of the Highland charge was revived as the 51st Highland Division earned the reputation of being the finest attacking division in the entire British army.

By 1918, Germany and her allies were exhausted, and forced to make peace. On all fronts, Britain and her Empire were triumphant, and many enemy colonies and territories were seized. By the peace treaties Britain received large acquisitions of territory, either as new possessions or under mandate to the newly-created League of Nations. The British Empire seemed more powerful than ever, for Britain's enemies had been crushed, and of her allies, France was utterly exhausted and Russia was convulsed by revolution.

51 Highland soldiers in the trenches, 1915.

Between the wars: the economy

But behind all these military successes and triumphs, Britain's real power and influence had been grievously diminished. In the later years of the nineteenth century, both Germany and the United States had overtaken her in industrial production, and now with the disruptions of the war Britain's position had been further eroded. Many traditional markets had been lost, for Britain had been unable to export goods during the war, and other countries had developed their own industries or had found new suppliers. Britain had also contracted huge debts to the United States, and she was forced to sell many of her overseas investments.

The years after 1918, therefore, were difficult ones for British industry. There was severe competition in foreign markets, especially as Germany and other countries recovered from the war, and Britain's share of the world's

52 A Scottish Hunger March passing through Northamptonshire, 1932.

exports fell steadily. At home during the 1920s, the total of unemployed frequently topped the one million mark, while labour relations were so bad that in 1926 there was a General Strike. In 1929 the British economy was rocked even further by a world-wide depression, and unemployment rose to a peak of almost 3 million in 1933. In an attempt to solve the crisis, the government abandoned its policy of free trade and instead placed duties on imports. But it was not until after 1935, when Britain began re-arming, that the situation was improved and the numbers of unemployed began significantly to fall.

Scotland was dependent on the heavy industries of shipbuilding, steel, engineering and mining, and she suffered severely during these dismal years. Shipbuilding, the growth industry of the pre-war years, was particularly affected, for as other countries developed their own industries, export orders collapsed. There was a short period of feverish activity immediately after the war as shipping losses were replaced, but from about 1929 the industry suffered a severe depression. Several yards were forced to halt production. Foreign owners stopped ordering ships from the Clyde because the costs were too high, and it was only when Admiralty orders for naval craft increased in the late 1930s that the position was improved.

Part of Scotland's difficulties lay in her failure to develop any of the new growth industries such as light engineering or car production. A few firms like the Argyll Company in Alexandria had built cars before and after the First

53 Deserted shipyards on Clydeside in the 1930s.

World War, but by the 1930s they had all failed. Meanwhile these industries were flourishing in the midlands and south-east of England, and these areas remained relatively prosperous while Scotland and the other regions dependent on heavy industries were suffering a savage depression.

And so it was that Scotland's economic position changed radically in the years after 1918. Whereas in the nineteenth century she had been one of the most prosperous regions of the leading industrial nation in the world, now she became one of the problem areas in a Britain that had herself lost her dominant position. Where before the initiative and skills of her managers and workers had kept her in the forefront of expansion and growth, now she was forced to seek and to accept assistance from the government. In the 1930s, for instance, the government provided assistance for the completion of the 81,000-ton *Queen Mary* at Clydebank, and helped build industrial estates suitable for light industries at Hillington near Glasgow and elsewhere. Such measures did bring some relief, but the basic imbalance of the Scottish economy remained.

Scottish farming also experienced difficulties after 1918. During the war, the farmers had been reasonably prosperous since foreign imports were largely cut off by U-boat attacks. They were asked to produce huge crops of potatoes, wheat and oats, and many acres of grassland were ploughed up. But after the war, imports of cheap foreign foodstuffs were resumed, and farmers were again crippled by this competition. During the 1930s, the government did alter its policy and began providing some assistance for farmers. It subsidised com-

54 The *Queen Mary* leaving Clydebank in 1936.

modities such as wheat and oats, and set up Marketing Boards to help the farmers obtain better prices for their products. Nevertheless, the total amount provided by the authorities was not very large, and many Scottish farmers had a hard struggle to keep going.

Scottish society

Scotland also faced serious social and welfare problems in the decades after 1918. Her housing was much poorer than the rest of the United Kingdom — in 1918, some 48 per cent of the people were living in one- or two-roomed houses as compared with only 7 per cent in England. A Royal Commission on Housing report issued in 1918 urged drastic action. During the next 20 years the government and local authorities did take positive steps to improve the situation. Various acts were passed giving local authorities the powers and the finances to build houses for rent, and subsidies were provided by the government to keep the rents at a reasonable level. In the 1920s and 1930s, large housing estates were built on the outskirts of the major towns and cities, and many families were rehoused in modern accommodation. Nevertheless, the housing problem in Scotland still remained acute. In 1939, many families were still living in slum conditions.

Scotland's health record during this period was also a dismal one. In the nineteenth century, the health and mortality rates had been generally similar to those in England, but by the 1920s Scotland had become one of the least healthy of all the countries in Western Europe. In 1936, for example, the infant mortality rate in Glasgow exceeded that for Oslo by 270 per cent and Stockholm by 290 per cent. The figures for maternal mortality (7 out of every 1,000) were a national disgrace, while tuberculosis was a terrible scourge, especially in the overcrowded houses of the industrial towns and cities. During the late 1930s there was some improvement in infant mortality rates, for example, but the overall position remained bleak.

Scotland was troubled by many other serious social problems and tensions in the decades after the First World War. Often these were connected with poor housing and environmental conditions, but the presence of large numbers of idle and unemployed youths in the industrial towns and cities added to the general difficulties. During the 1920s and 1930s, several rival gangs were active in Glasgow and other towns. From time to time they fought pitched battles in the main streets and thoroughfares, causing terror and disruption. Glasgow earned an evil reputation as the infamous 'No Mean City', and certain of its districts such as the Gorbals became quite notorious. In the towns of the west, too, economic and social troubles were intensified by religious rivalry between the Irish 'Orange' and 'Green' factions — these also became closely associated with the famous Glasgow football clubs, Rangers and Celtic.

Life in Scotland's industrial towns and cities was not all gang fights, illness and violence, however. In the great tenements of Glasgow and other places, a fascinating social life had evolved. Each little street formed a real living community. With their 'steamies', the football and the public houses, the citizens managed to inject some drama and colour into their lives. The children, for their part, had a rich folk culture of street songs and verse to enjoy. They

55 *Above* Typical street scene in the Gorbals.

56 *Below* A Rangers *v* Celtic match at Ibrox Stadium, Glasgow, 1949.

had also many wonderful places to explore, and a wide range of games and other activities. Molly Weir, a famous Scottish radio personality, has given a vivid picture of life in Glasgow in this period. She shows how the children could even receive a valuable dramatic training in their 'backgreen' performances:

> We charged a ha'penny for children and a penny for adults, and the adults sat on the stone edging which ran round the back-court railings. The children sat on the ground or stood, just as they pleased. We generally gave two performances, and our audience usually stayed for both, and were highly critical if they didn't get an exact repeat performance at the second house, word for word, gesture for gesture.
>
> I was quite drunk with power when I discovered how easy it was to change the mood of an audience from one of enthusiastic noisy delight at my swash-buckling impersonation of a Principal Boy, to silent pathos at my rendering of 'Won't you buy my pretty flowers'.

Above all, perhaps, there was the cinema. The first movies had been produced just before the First World War, and during the 1920s and 1930s every district came to have its local picture-house. Each Saturday, hordes of children would pour forth from their tenement homes to attend the matinée performance. A nominal charge would secure admission, and then they would watch enthralled as their cowboys and other heroes performed superhuman epics, and were left at the end of each week's instalment in an impossible predicament. All week the youngsters would suffer an agony of suspense, but on the following Saturday they would discover that the hero had made his escape by some miraculous and ingenious means.

Politics

The social problems of the industrial towns had a close connection with political developments between 1918 and 1939. After the First World War, the Labour Party won increasing support from the British public. In 1924 and 1929, it formed minority governments under a Scottish Prime Minister, Ramsay MacDonald. The Depression helped to split the Labour Government and bring in a Conservative-dominated National government in 1931, and this government remained in office until the outbreak of the Second World War in 1939. Nevertheless, the Labour Party still remained the main opposition – by this time, it had clearly replaced the Liberal Party as one of the two major parties in Britain.

The general pattern of Scottish politics followed the trends evident in the rest of the country, but there was a tendency for the Labour Party to be in a stronger position in Scotland. After 1918, the working classes of the industrial belt came increasingly to support the Labour Party, and steadily it gained control of the industrial constituencies. During the 1920s, too, a group of MPs from Clydeside and nearby areas in Central Scotland won a considerable reputation for their militant and fiery speeches, and for their radical demands. This period between the wars also saw the appearance of a political

57 A meeting of the Scottish Nationalists in 1939.

nationalist movement in Scotland. At first, the Labour Party had favoured Home Rule for Scotland, and Scottish Labour MPs introduced several unsuccessful Home Rule Bills into Parliament. The failure of these bills brought about the formation of a National Party in 1928. In 1934 this and other groups joined together to form the Scottish National Party. The SNP sought Home Rule, but it failed to make much impact in elections, and its candidates generally lost their deposits. There was some support for its policies in the universities and among writers and artists, but it made almost no impression among the working classes in the industrial constituencies.

The development of the Scottish National Party and the nationalist movement had been in part a product of a literary revival in Scotland led by such writers as Hugh MacDiarmid and Neil Gunn. Hugh MacDiarmid wrote poetry of the highest quality, and he sought to create a true Scots language which would be a proper vehicle for a restored and revitalized Scottish culture. Another writer of the period, Lewis Grassic Gibbon, wrote in a specially contrived Anglo-Scots, and used this in several novels to evoke the life of various Scottish communities. Neil Gunn was a major literary figure, and in a series of wonderful novels he drew upon the whole Scottish tradition, both Lowland and Gaelic, to explore and answer the fundamental problems and dilemmas of men in modern Scotland. Such writers and their works were evidence of an awakening national consciousness in Scotland. For many critics and observers, this was perhaps the most significant development of the inter-war period.

58 Hugh MacDiarmid, the Scottish poet who headed the literary revival in Scotland in the years between the wars.

The Second World War

The years between 1918 and 1939 were not on the whole good ones for Scotland. Her economy suffered a serious reverse, and she was faced with complex problems in health, housing and other social spheres. Much of the old confidence in the country's destiny was lost. But in 1939, Scotland was once again caught up in a great conflict that seemed to overshadow all other considerations. During the 1930s, Germany was governed by Adolf Hitler and his National Socialist Party. Soon they had embarked on a campaign to win back all the territories which Germany lost in 1918. In September 1939, German troops marched into Poland. Britain and France had promised to support Poland in such an eventuality, and so declared war on Germany. The Second World War had begun. As in 1914, the British Empire rallied to support the mother country, and once again Scotland and the Scottish regiments prepared to play their full part.

In the early stages of the war, Germany won great victories. She invaded and defeated France, and overran many other countries in Europe. In 1941, she invaded Russia and occupied great stretches of territory. Later in 1941 she was joined by Japan, and the United States was brought into the war on the side of Britain. The Japanese, too, achieved tremendous successes, and they occupied many British possessions in South-East Asia. But after 1942 the tide of war turned. Germany was pressed back within her own borders by Russian, American and British forces. Finally, in 1945, she was forced to surrender. In the east the Japanese were also driven back. In August 1945, two atomic bombs were dropped on Japan, and she, too, surrendered.

9. Scotland at the Cross-Roads

Post-war Britain

After 1945 and the end of the Second World War, serious efforts were made in Britain to prevent a recurrence of the depressions and large-scale unemployment that had marked the years between 1918 and 1939. Several of the major industries such as coal mining, the railways and the electricity supply were nationalized, and the various governments pursued policies of full employment. Over the years there was a steady increase in production, and in certain industries like the car industry output soared to record heights. British farming also increased its yields. By 1973, it was turning out 60 per cent of the food consumed in the entire country, as compared with only 30 per cent before 1939. In 1948, the government had introduced a support system whereby farmers received subsidies and had guaranteed prices and markets for their produce, but cheap foreign foodstuffs were still allowed entry to keep down the cost of food for the housewives.

By and large, these various policies brought increased prosperity to the people of the United Kingdom in post-war years. Wages and the standard of living rose very considerably, and people became accustomed to washing machines, refrigerators, television sets and many other luxury domestic appliances. The number of car owners rose dramatically, while the development of air travel and charter flights brought holidays abroad within the reach of almost all sections of the community. Nor had the less fortunate been forgotten, for a comprehensive welfare state was introduced to provide skilled medical treatment, family allowances and maternity benefits for all, and social security benefits for those unable to work or whose income fell below a basic minimum level.

Nevertheless, despite all these improvements and advances, Britain's economic performance after 1945 did not compare at all favourably with other industrial countries. While her national production rose slowly and steadily, that of Germany, Japan, the United States, France, Italy and almost all the major developed countries increased very much faster. Repeatedly, too, Britain experienced balance of payments crises as her imports exceeded her exports. Frequently the government was forced to hold back production in order to correct the deficiencies. Slowly, Britain slipped further and further back in her relative world position. By 1973, almost all the countries of Western Europe had achieved greater productivity and a higher standard of living.

This relatively unimpressive performance by Britain was a vital factor in bringing about her entry into the European Economic Community. Initially Britain, with her Empire and large imperial trade, had decided to remain outside when the six countries of Germany, France, Italy, Belgium, Holland

and Luxembourg formed the Common Market in 1957. But during the 1960s, many government ministers and industrialists came to favour entry into this large, powerful economic unit as a solution to Britain's problems. After two unsuccessful applications, she was finally admitted in 1973.

Scotland and the Scottish economy

Basically Scotland has shared the same economic and social experiences as·the rest of the United Kingdom since 1945. Her problems, however, have been. even more severe and deep-seated. The standard of living has risen, but housing and health have continued to present greater problems than in England. Extensive programmes of house-building have been initiated, and most of the slums have been cleared; but in Glasgow and some other industrial towns there are still several black spots where conditions and the quality of life are quite unsatisfactory.

59 Contrast between new flats and old in the Gorbals, Glasgow.

In the economic sphere, Scotland's main difficulty has been the continued dominance of older industries such as engineering, shipbuilding, steel and mining. These industries have experienced a steady decline in the post-war years, and this has been a factor in keeping the Scottish rate of unemployment at a figure almost double the United Kingdom average. There has also been a steady flow of people out of the country looking for employment elsewhere. In some years as many as 40,000 people emigrated from Scotland. The days when Scotland was one of the major growth areas of the industrial world are long since past, and increasingly she is being considered a problem region in the British economy.

Nowhere perhaps is the sad decline of the Scottish economy more clearly illustrated than in the shipbuilding industry. After 1945 there was a short boom as wartime losses were replaced, but soon the Scottish shipyards were experiencing intense competition from such countries as Germany and Japan. By 1968, several of the companies on the Upper Clyde were in serious difficulties, and the government provided finance and support for a new group called Upper Clyde Shipbuilders. This new company also ran into difficulties, and in 1971 the government withdrew its support and began planning closures. This was resisted by a 'work-in' of the labour force, and eventually a somewhat smaller, government-backed company known as Govan Shipbuilders was set up. The Scott-Lithgow Company on the Lower Clyde was more successful, and was able to build giant modern ships at competitive prices. Nevertheless, Scott-Lithgow's, as well as Govan Shipbuilders and the other surviving companies, will continue to face fierce foreign competition in the years ahead, and they will survive only if their yards can become increasingly efficient and productive.

To compensate for the decline in shipbuilding and other heavy industries, attempts have been made in post-war years to secure for Scotland a share in some of the more prosperous and expanding industries. There have been important developments in electronics with Ferranti at Edinburgh and Honeywell Controls at Newhouse, in business machinery with National Cash Register at Dundee and IBM at Greenock, and in petro-chemicals at Grangemouth. The government has also adopted regional policies aimed at stimulating new enterprises. Grants, tax concessions and other inducements have been given to firms setting up in Scotland, and at times government pressure has been directed at large firms to persuade them to move up north. In this way a truck and tractor factory was established by BMC (later British Leyland) at Bathgate in 1961, while in 1963 a car factory was opened by Rootes (later Chrysler) at Linwood near Paisley. All this has helped achieve a better balance in the Scottish economy, but the arrival of new jobs and enterprises has not quite made up for the loss of older forms of work and industries.

Government grants and assistance have also been directed towards solving the long-standing Highland problem in Scotland. The Crofters' Act of 1886 had certainly safeguarded the position of crofters and smallholders, but the population of the Highlands continued to decline throughout the first half of the twentieth century. In 1965, the government decided to set up a Highlands and Islands Development Board charged with the task of revitalizing the area. It

60 *Above* The Forth Road Bridge, opened in 1964.

61 *Below* Skiers setting off from Aviemore to the Cairngorms.

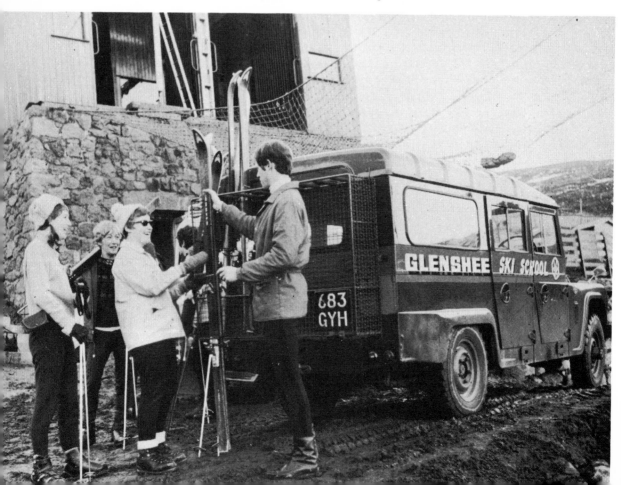

was given considerable powers and a budget of a few million pounds a year, and since its inception it has achieved some successes. It has, for instance, been involved in bringing a wood pulp mill to Fort William, and in setting up an aluminium smelter on the Cromarty Firth. It has also co-operated with the Scottish Tourist Board to stimulate tourism, and grants have been given for new hotels, and also for winter sports, sea angling and other imaginative projects. The 1971 census revealed that all this had had some effect — the long decline in the population of the region had been halted and even reversed. Unfortunately, however, depopulation has continued in the islands and rural areas, and it is only in towns like Inverness that real advances have been made.

The discovery in 1970 of rich oilfields off the Scottish north-east coast and in the waters near the Shetland Islands injected a new factor into the Scottish economic situation, Highlands and Lowlands alike. In a relatively short time, the economy of Aberdeen and other east coast areas has been transformed as oil operators have flooded into the region to exploit the new discoveries. New yards for constructing rigs and platforms have been opened in Fife, Clydeside and the Cromarty Firth, and there has been a considerable spin-off in service, financial and other activities.

Quite clearly the new oil resources promise much, and they could help to restore the Scottish economy to the position of relative prosperity and dominance it held in the nineteenth century. Nevertheless, there are many Scots who fear that their country will not obtain the full benefits of this development. The oil royalties are under the control of the British government, and in effect the authorities have given considerable powers and freedom to the

62 An oil drilling platform off the Shetlands, 1972.

international oil companies. The main profits and benefits of the oil technology have so far gone to American companies, while the Scottish firms have generally been active only in the supply and supporting industries.

Politics

The government's handling of this new source of wealth has become one of the main issues in Scottish politics in the 1970s. For most of the years from 1945, the political scene was dominated by the Labour and Conservative Parties, as it was in the United Kingdom as a whole, with rival governments alternating as the balance of power swung one way and then the other. In Scotland, however, the Labour Party tended to have a much more dominant position than in England, while the Liberal Party also had a proportionately large representation, particularly in the Highlands and Border areas.

In the 1960s, a new political force emerged in Scotland in the guise of a reinvigorated Scottish National Party. In the 1950s there had been some revival of interest in Home Rule — a Scottish Covenant asking for devolution received over 2 million signatures. The SNP, however, made little impact at election time. Then in the early 1960s the membership of the SNP began to increase dramatically. After a series of good results in by-elections at West Lothian and Glasgow Pollock, they won their first by-election at Hamilton in 1967. They

63 Mrs Winifred Ewing, the Scottish Nationalist victor in the Hamilton by-election, 1967.

lost Hamilton, but gained the Western Isles at the General Election of 1970, and in subsequent years maintained their challenge. In 1973, they came close to winning a by-election at Dundee, and later in the year they won the previously safe Labour seat at Govan. Part of their success was undoubtedly due to their demand that the revenues from Scottish oil should go to Scotland — their policies in this sphere seem to have evoked considerable response from the Scottish electorate.

The activities of the SNP forced the other parties to display a greater interest in Scottish affairs. The Conservatives, for instance, brought forward proposals for a Scottish Assembly, but these were for discussion only, and not for immediate implementation. In 1967, too, the Labour Government set up a Commission to investigate the whole constitutional position. Its report, the Kilbrandon Report, was issued in November, 1973. The majority of the Commission's members supported a proposal for the setting up of Assemblies in Scotland and Wales, which would be responsible for such areas as education, housing, and the police. The Report met with a certain amount of criticism and opposition. However, taken in conjunction with the SNP victory at Govan, it indicated that the whole question of political devolution in Scotland was a very real and pressing one.

Scottish life and culture

The growing interest in things Scottish on the political scene reflects perhaps a continuing revival of Scottish culture since 1945. The Scottish 'renaissance' initiated by such writers as Hugh MacDiarmid in the inter-war years has been carried on by authors like George Mackay Brown and Ian Crichton Smith. Particularly noteworthy are a group of novels about life in the industrial towns and cities of Scotland by writers like Archie Hind and Alan Sharp — they have created a vivid and faithful picture of working-class people in their homes and their ordinary environment.

This appearance of quality Scottish literature based on life in the industrial towns is perhaps one of the most important developments in modern Scotland. The Industrial Revolution brought large numbers of people from Ireland, the Highlands and the rural areas into the towns and cities of the Lowlands, and over the years a new type of town-dwelling, industrial Scot had evolved. Some groups like the Irish resisted assimilation for a period, but it would now appear that the process of assimilation is nearing completion. Previously no Scottish writer could produce anything but cardboard caricatures of the working-class inhabitants of Glasgow and other industrial towns, but now that the modern Scot can be identified much more easily, writers and artists are able to portray him in all his rich complexity.

Other illustrations of a revival of Scottish culture are to be seen in the achievements of the highly successful Scottish National Orchestra, and the founding of a Scottish Opera Company which has already won very considerable international fame. Strong pressures have also been exerted towards the setting up of a Scottish National Theatre which would enhance the quality of dramatic art in Scotland. And in 1946, the authorities in Edinburgh launched the International Edinburgh Festival, which has become one of the world's

64 The Edinburgh Military Tattoo.

major festivals of music and drama.

Important developments have also taken place in other aspects of the country's cultural and social life. The Church of Scotland and other churches still retain an important position, but they have declined both in their membership and in their general influence. Scottish education has witnessed a remarkable revolution — new progressive methods, curricula and examinations have appeared, and pupils have been given a much wider range of school subjects. There has also been an extension of out-of-school activities, and Scottish children now participate in mountaineering, skiing, sailing and a host of other outdoor pursuits. An increasing number of adults are also engaging in these varied activities. For the majority of working-class people, however, association football and the regular clashes between Rangers and Celtic still continue to hold pride of place.

The future of Scotland
Despite the many fascinating developments that have affected Scotland in the post-war era, the mood of the Scottish people as a whole is a deeply questioning one. In a sense, all the old certainties have vanished — the economic and political realities that shaped Scotland's destiny for more than 250 years have been undermined. With the Act of Union, England and Scotland

joined together to create a new economic prosperity and build up a world-wide empire. With the passing of that empire and the loss of economic supremacy, something of the old purpose has gone. Since 1945, Britain has granted independence to almost every one of her former colonies. The imperial vision that took Scots to every corner of the world and caused them to submerge their lives in a greater identity is dimmed. Even as Britain has been forced to seek a new purposeful role in the European Community, so inevitably Scotland has been forced to consider her own function within this new grouping.

No-one of course can predict with any certainty what course the people of Scotland will follow at this cross-roads in their history. There is little doubt, however, that the present questioning mood could produce some readjustments of the old landmarks. The links with England and the United Kingdom are still very strong, but it seems likely that the relationship will in time be subtly changed. The report of the Kilbrandon Commission on the constitution could well provide the necessary impetus for giving Scotland a separate Assembly, and produce further devolution of government and administration.

An important factor in determining the future of the Scottish people will undoubtedly be the performance of their economy. In 1707, economic needs and the desire for entry into English and colonial markets decisively influenced the actions of Scottish politicians. Clearly economic considerations will be equally important in determining future developments in Scotland. The relatively poor performance of the Scottish economy since 1914 has been one important factor in producing demands for change. A continuing situation

65 An oil tanker discharging oil at the Finnart Ocean Terminal, Loch Long.

where it seemed as if Scotland must remain in an inferior position would undoubtedly strengthen demands for devolution and independence.

The economic prospects for Scotland are rather difficult to estimate. The discovery of oilfields in the North Sea is promising, while the advantages Scotland enjoys with her deep-water sites on the west coast and her strategic geographical position are extremely encouraging. These latter aspects have given rise to the 'Oceanspan' proposals whereby Scotland would form a land bridge for trade between the Americas and Europe. Giant tankers and other ships would bring raw materials and goods to places like Hunterston on the Ayrshire coast, and they would then be transported across central Scotland for shipment to the Continent. Along this land corridor, associated industries could process the raw material, while on the convenient site at Hunterston a great new steel complex would make Scotland a leading industrial power once again. But at present the Scots have no real control over such plans, and they must first persuade and convince the authorities in London that they are worthwhile and feasible. It is to be hoped that all these dreams will not be shattered, and that the growing optimism will not turn to anger and frustration under the existing constitutional arrangements.

Conclusion

Whatever course is followed by Scotland and the Scots in the future, it is certain that several vital and enduring features of the national story will continue. Through all ages, the Scots have been faced with the seemingly eternal problems of wresting a living from an uncertain environment, and of arranging their relations with their more powerful neighbour to the south. At various times they have favoured different solutions, but through all the changes and revolutions there has been a continuity and a tradition which is the living essence of the Scottish people. And always this living tradition and community have been shaped and moulded by the land of Scotland, so that in a very real sense the story of the Scottish people is the story of Scotland herself. Even as the Scottish people move into a new age and a new destiny, we can be certain that their future will be shaped by the living past, and by the enduring reality that is Scotland.

Table of Dates

Further Reading

J Buchan, *Montrose* (Hodder and Stoughton, 1949).
R H Campbell, *Scotland since 1707* (Basil Blackwell, 1965).
W Croft Dickinson, *Scotland from Earliest Times to 1603* (Nelson, 1961).
G Donaldson, *Scotland: James V to James VII* (Oliver and Boyd, 1965).
W Fergusson, *Scotland: 1689 to the Present* (Oliver and Boyd, 1968).
M Gray, *The Highland Economy 1750-1850* (Oliver and Boyd, 1957).
R L Mackie, *A Short History of Scotland* (Oliver and Boyd, 1962).
F MacLean, *A Concise History of Scotland* (Thames and Hudson, 1970).
G Menzies, editor, *Who are the Scots?* (BBC Publication, 1971).
R Mitchison, *A History of Scotland* (Methuen, 1970).
J Prebble, *The Lion in the North* (Secker and Warburg, 1971).
G S Pryde, *Scotland from 1603 to the Present Day* (Nelson, 1968).
T C Smout, *A History of the Scottish People 1560-1830* (Collins, 1969).

Fiction
G M Brown, *An Orkney Tapestry* (Gollancz, 1969).
J Galt, *Annals of the Parish* (OUP, 1972).
Lewis Grassic Gibbon, *A Scots Quair* (Hutchinson, 1966).
N M Gunn, *The Silver Darlings* (Faber, 1969).
N M Gunn, *Morning Tide* (Faber, 1931).
Sir Walter Scott, *Waverley* (Dent, 1969).
Sir Walter Scott, *Guy Mannering* (Dent, 1963).
Sir Walter Scott, *The Heart of Midlothian* (Collins, 1952).
Sir Walter Scott, *Rob Roy* (Dent, 1963).
Sir Walter Scott, *Old Mortality* (Dent, 1969).
A Sharp, *A Green Tree in Gedde* (Michael Joseph, 1965).
Ian C Smith, *Consider the Lilies* (Gollancz, 1968).
R L Stevenson, *Kidnapped* (Collins, 1952).
R L Stevenson, *Catriona* (Collins, 1952).
R L Stevenson, *The Master of Ballantrae* (Collins, 1952).

Index

Numbers in **bold** refer to the figure numbers of the illustrations.